THE MESSAGE OF THE
OLD TESTAMENT

THE MESSAGE OF THE OLD TESTAMENT

H.L. ELLISON

THE PATERNOSTER PRESS
Carlisle UK

British Library Cataloguing-in-Publication Data

A catalogue record for this book
is available from the British Library.

ISBN 0–85364–606–6

Typeset by Photoprint, Torquay, Devon
and printed in the UK for
The Paternoster Press
P.O. Box 300, Carlisle, Cumbria, CA3 0QS
by Cox and Wyman Ltd, Reading

Contents

For

NANCY

RUTH

ELISABETH

who think their father's books

worth reading

Preface

IT IS ALWAYS USUAL TO BLAME THE PAST FOR THE TROUBLES OF THE present. There are many who throw scorn on their fathers and grandfathers for allowing the 'higher critics' to rob them of their trust in the truth and value of the Bible and especially of the Old Testament.

Of higher critics, like all human movements, both good and evil may be said, but it cannot be denied that they are largely to blame for present-day lack of interest in and knowledge of the Old Testament. All too often they turned the thoughts of the young away from what the Bible had to say to information and theories about the Bible. But the critics of the critics forget that their fathers and grandfathers fell a prey to the new ideas just because they did not know much about the Old Testament.

Of the critics and their ways there is nothing in this little book, though it could not have been written without them. Its one aim is to make it a little easier for a younger generation to read the Old Testament somewhat more intelligently. That is why there is no list of works for further reading or of Bible helps, for its one purpose is to turn its readers to the Bible itself. Those who do wish further information and help should not find it hard to obtain.

The bulk of this book appeared in *The Witness*, a monthly published by Messrs Pickering & Inglis.

H.L. ELLISON

ONE

The Problem of the Old Testament

PAUL WAS WRITING WHAT HE KNEW WAS ALMOST CERTAINLY HIS farewell letter to the man he loved above all his other converts. He reminded Timothy of what he had learnt from his grandmother Lois and mother Eunice and then from him, Paul. He stressed especially the value 'the sacred writings' (the Old Testament) had been to him (2 Tim. 3: 15). They 'have power to make you wise and lead you to salvation through faith in Christ Jesus' (NEB). But that is not all. 'All scripture is inspired by God and profitable for teaching, for reproof, for correction, and for training in righteousness, that the man of God may be complete, equipped for every good work.'

What was Paul's purpose in adding these words? If we may judge by what is spoken and written, most of us are mainly interested in 'all scripture is inspired by God'. There is no harm in this, because it is just this quality of inspiration that makes the Bible speak to every age and generation, even though circumstances and needs change. Living, as we do, in a time when the reality of inspiration is widely denied, we have every right to appeal to Paul's testimony. But since hardly anyone in his day denied the inspiration of the Old Testament, this was clearly not the idea uppermost in his thoughts.

On this passage that great, American, conservative scholar B. B. Warfield wrote: 'There is room for some difference of opinion as to the exact construction of this declaration. Shall we render "Every (or all) Scripture is God-breathed and (therefore) profitable," or "Every (or all) Scripture, being God-breathed, is as well profitable"? . . . In both cases these Sacred Scriptures are declared to owe their value to their Divine origin; and in both cases this their Divine origin is energetically asserted of their entire fabric. On the whole, the preferable construction would seem to be, "Every Scripture, seeing that it is God-breathed, is as well profitable." In that case, what the apostle asserts is that the Sacred Scriptures, in their every several passage . . . is the product of the creative breath of God, and because of this its Divine origination, is of supreme value for all holy purposes.'[1]

Few will doubt this judgment, that here the inspiration of Scripture is being stressed as a guarantee of the practical value of every part. But how few of us even try to find a use in every part of the Old Testament. Scripture, as Paul used it, did not refer to the slowly forming canon of the New Testament but to the Old. Of course the same is true of the New, but the fact of the New has not decreased the value of the Old.

Many would suggest that this is too severe a judgment and that at least certain parts of the Old Testament are widely and constantly used. Each reader can check the value of such a statement by noting how often he hears the Old Testament used in the next six months. The check will be of the more value, if he also notes what portions were used. A refreshing exception is provided by those 'old-fashioned' churches where one sermon a Sunday, generally that during the morning worship, is taken from the Old Testament. In fact, if we leave attempts to forecast the future to one side, the commonest uses are typological or allegorical. The former, though entirely justified, when there is really a type in the passage, generally needs the New Testament before we can find it, while the latter is entirely dependent on the New Testament revelation.[2] So both, while using the Old, virtually deny its lasting value. As one young man said after listening to a 'gospel sermon' based on the story of Joseph and the butler and baker, 'It was true, but it could have been expressed so much more simply without them'. What Paul wrote to

[1] ISBE, article 'inspiration', reprinted in *The Inspiration and Authority of the Bible*, page 134.
[2] For the difference between allegory and typology see Appendix I.

Timothy was that the Christian worker – but one has to know
the gospel story before one can be a Christian! – can on the
basis of the Old Testament alone obtain all the instruction he
needs for his own life and for teaching others how to live.

The Old Testament is not a preparation for the New, but
the major portion of one revelation by God. The Old is
incomplete without the New, for in all its portions it is looking
forward to its fulfilment, but the New is also incomplete
without the Old. To use it alone is like taking the roofs and
towers of a great cathedral in isolation and suggesting that
the walls exist only that they may bear the roof.

THE DIFFICULTIES OF THE OLD TESTAMENT

Why is it that we do not appreciate the Old Testament in the
way Paul did? Many reasons may be suggested. The world
and thought-life of the Old are far further separated from our
experience than are those of the New.[3] Then some of the
outstanding pages of the Old are among the worst translated
in the AV, so that it becomes a major effort to understand
them. This is a valid difficulty only for those who accept the
virtual inspiration of the AV. RV and even more RSV remove
most, though not all, translational difficulties. More important is the length of the Old, over three times that of the New.
The outstanding skill of the modern printer tends to obscure
this from us and make us think that it is much shorter than it
is. This can, however, be exaggerated. The various Bible-
reading plans by which the whole Bible is covered in a year
make no intolerable calls on the person with some degree of
leisure.

The deepest reason is that there is no obvious unifying
principle in the Old Testament. When he has to teach a large
number of facts, the good teacher tries to link them together
in one way or another, finding some logical link between
them. But it is just this that the normal reader of the Old
Testament finds so hard to discover.

So very much has been written on the Old Testament

---

[3] The main difference is its greater simplicity and concreteness. That
is why children, in spite of the views of some modern educationalists,
often understand the *stories* of the Old Testament better than their
parents.

through the centuries, but how little has really satisfied or made it a living book. Most have approached it from the New Testament and they have found it full of fingers pointing to Jesus the Messiah. They have followed in the footsteps of their Master, who on the way to Emmaus 'beginning with Moses and all the prophets interpreted to them in all the scriptures the things concerning Himself'. Their spirits have been stirred in them, but when they have finished, they must have felt that much of the Old Testament had refused to yield up its meaning.

Others have followed in the footsteps of the writer to the Hebrews. They have not always heeded the subtle warning conveyed by, 'Of these things we cannot now speak in detail' (Heb. 9: 5). Above all they have all too often not followed his movement of thought. He began with the Old and from it directed his readers' gaze to the greater glories of the Christ. We, more often than not, decide from our study of the New what the truth is, and then force the Old to echo our thoughts. But even where we have handled these Scriptures aright, we must often have been left with the uneasy feeling that the Old had not revealed to us all its secrets.

Others have spent years of devoted study on those sections of the Old which in fact or appearance look forward to a future yet ahead of us, and then they have woven them together with similar passages from the New. More than ever they awaken the feeling that the true spiritual content has gone lost on the way. What is even more disappointing to men of true spiritual insight, they find that they have failed to find agreement with other devout persons treading the same path.

Yet others in their deep conviction that every part of the Old must have its message for them, try to force it to yield it up by adopting the methods of allegory, of saying that it means not what it seems to, but something quite other. This may flatter our ingenuity, but it will seldom feed us with the pure milk of the word.

THE VARIOUS STRANDS OF THE OLD TESTAMENT

The simple fact is that the Old Testament consists of a number of strands which have never been woven or fused together. They are a harmony, but certainly not a unity. They do come together in the focal point provided by Jesus Christ, but that point lies outside its bounds, and we must not provide it too quickly. We must be prepared to explore how far any of the Old Testament strands will take us before we pass its limits.[4]

I have often been asked whether Isaiah knew that King Immanuel of Isa. 7: 1–4; 9: 2–7; 11: 1–9 was the same as the Servant of Jehovah of Isa. 42: 1–4; 49: 1–6; 50: 4–9; 52: 13–53: 12. I have always replied, 'I do not know; but there is no reason why he should have. Certainly there is no evidence that he taught his disciples so.' This method of putting side by side is part of the sundry ways and divers manners in God's revelation that the Epistle to the Hebrews speaks of.

If we were to try to enumerate all these strands, we should be in danger of making differences which the Holy Spirit never made, but the main ones are easy enough to enumerate.

There is first the early history of creation and mankind in general, Gen. 1–11. We rightly feel that these chapters are basic for revelation, yet how seldom, how very seldom, are they referred to in the books that follow. Much the same is true of the story of the patriarchs that fills the remaining chapters of Genesis. Certain points recur from time to time, but the spiritual lessons which we take for granted are not often mentioned in the books that follow.

What are we to say then of the history from the Exodus to the work of Ezra and Nehemiah? Closer study will probably convince us that here too we should divide into strands. There is the story of God's deliverance, which brought the people from the bondage of Egypt to the borders of the Promised Land. Then there is the great 'Deuteronomic history' from the fulfilment of God's promise to the disappearance of the Jewish state as Nebuchadnezzar laid waste city and temple. Finally the story is partially retold and carried on in Chronicles, Ezra, Nehemiah, Esther but with a subtly different slant. This division is no arbitrary one, for in the Hebrew Bible, with its

---

[4] It is a well-known fact that those modern theologies of the Old Testament which seek a unifying factor within it have never really done justice to all the strands that make it up.

different order of books, the first is in the Law, the second in the Prophets, and the last in the Writings.[5]

We may think too of the various subdivisions of the Law. Not only is there the clear subdivision into moral and ritual or cultic, but in the moral itself we have varying emphases between the Book of the Covenant (Ex. 20-23), the Law of Holiness (Lev. 17-26) and the Deuteronomic Code (Deut. 5, 12-30). This is not to say that the dividing line between moral and ritual is always clearly drawn.

If we do no more than compare the messages of Amos and Hosea, we shall realize how the Spirit of God spoke along different lines to His servants the prophets, although they harmonize in Christ. Again there was much spoken mainly to the prophets' own generation which found its fulfilment in it, and other oracles which looked to the future, and could hope for no fulfilment until the Coming One should come.

Books like Proverbs, Job and Ecclesiastes are not merely disparate, when compared with each other, but breathe an atmosphere which is rare in the rest of the Old Testament. Finally, where are we to fit in works like Lamentations and the Song of Songs? The Psalter has more variety of outlook than even a modern hymn book.

If such is the many-coloured variety and wonder of the Old Testament, it is easy enough to understand why one approach alone will fail to unlock all its riches to us. Every strand will lead us sooner or later to Christ or to a need for Him, but this will not be achieved by trying short cuts. If we allow the Holy Spirit to lead us along the strands of His revelation, we shall find our Lord at the last yet more wonderful than we had realized Him to be.

The purpose of this book is to take the various strands in turn in order to explore what facet of Divine revelation each has to offer.

[5] See Appendix II.

TWO

The Primæval Revelation

WE ARE TOLD BY JOHN THAT 'THE TRUE LIGHT THAT ENLIGHTENS every man was coming into the world' (John 1: 9), but apart from the statement of Rom. 1: 19, 20 the Bible gives us little more than hints as to what knowledge this enlightenment may bring with it. It is not unreasonable, however, to see in Gen. 1–11 an outline of that basic knowledge that man should have of God, quite apart from the revelation contained in the Bible.

I am making no suggestion that the literary form of these chapters is earlier than Abraham. However we may imagine, for know we never can, the way in which the revelation of Gen. 1: 1–2: 3 was given, there is no evidence whatever that it ever existed in any other language before Hebrew, and there are few conservatives who would attribute it to a lesser figure than Moses. The position is other, when we turn to the other stories in these chapters, viz. Eden, the fall, the flood and the Tower of Babel. There are grounds, linguistic and others, for thinking that Abram brought them with him, not necessarily in written form, when he came into Canaan from Haran, and that they go far back long before his time. To avoid misunderstanding, let me stress that while I believe they are in essence the world's oldest stories, yet in the form we have them in the Bible they are as much the result of the Holy Spirit's inspirational activity as any other part of Scripture. I am not prepared to argue the possible but unprovable assertion that only among the ancestors of Abram were these stories preserved in pure form but merely that the Holy Spirit saw to it that in their recording all error was eliminated. That awaited their being written.

When we look at these stories without going into detail, we see that they teach the existence of a creator God and of a golden age. This was ended by the fault of man, which made a barrier between him and God. This was followed by rapid moral deterioration, which ended with an outstanding judgment by God. Finally God placed the punishment of futility on man, so that he should never achieve his purposes, thanks to the division between man and man, nation and nation.

Many books have been written to show that these truths, though not necessarily these stories, belong to the heritage of the human race. Sometimes they have become atrophied, sometimes they have taken on strange, twisted forms, which make the original truth almost unrecognizable, but they have provided some point of contact, when the truth of Christ has been proclaimed.

ITS PLACE IN THE OLD TESTAMENT

We are not concerned with the history of these truths among the nations. Paul tells us how they reacted to the standing revelation of God in nature (Rom. 1: 19–23), and so the memories of the primaeval past also lost whatever power they might have possessed. Gen. 1–11 stand in the Bible as an integral and essential part of the story of redemption, and this is our concern here.

The chronological figures of these chapters are nowhere else referred to in the Bible, and except for 1 Chr. 1, the genealogical details are referred to rarely and almost casually, e.g. Jude 14. The detailed genealogies of our Lord in Matt. 1, Lk. 3 have obviously another purpose. We may conclude then, that however much the genealogies in Gen. 1–11 may act as an invitation to some to work out the chronology of earth's early ages, they were not recorded for this purpose in the first place.

The Bible deals with a mere fraction of the earth's surface, and only a few of its peoples and rulers find mention in it. These genealogies and attendant figures should serve as a guarantee to us that there has been no age of man and no area of the earth's surface that has not been under God's rule. The very word of God that proclaims His choice of Israel, 'Now therefore, if you will obey My voice and keep My covenant, you shall be My own possession among all peoples', also affirms His universal rule 'for all the earth is Mine' (Ex. 19: 5). So the genealogies served to remind Israel, and later the Church, that the world does not exist purely on their behalf, and God's providential care is not confined to them.

When we remove the genealogies from Gen. 1–11, we are left with the stories already enumerated; the truths enshrined in them become the background and an essential part of the explanation of all that follows. While they gain in depth as the revelation of God broadens until it reaches its fulness in Christ, they never lose their primary position in Scripture. It comes then as somewhat a surprise to find that they are apparently so seldom referred to in the steadily unrolling revelation through the centuries.

THE FLOOD AND BABEL

It is on the face of it extraordinary that the story of the Tower of Babel does not seem to be referred to elsewhere in the Bible, and the story of the Flood but seldom. Closer investigation will show that this impression is misleading.

For our purpose it is irrelevant whether some of the mentions of Babylon in Revelation refer to the historic city, which, as some affirm, is yet to be rebuilt, or whether they are all metaphorical. It is assumed that the spiritual meaning will be obvious to the reader. The metaphorical use of Babylon was not very common among the earlier rabbis, so there is no question of its being interpreted by ordinary Jewish usage. The Old Testament, however, makes it clear.

Isaiah's prophecies against the nations begin with a prophecy about the fall of Babylon (ch. 13), which seems to have no connection with his own time and which hardly links with the predictions of chs. 40–55. Clearly it links rather with the Day of the Lord. It is followed by a taunt song over 'the king of Babylon' (14: 3–20), who remains unidentified. Indeed we should almost lose, if we could put a name to him. We really capture the meaning of these oracles, when we grasp that for Isaiah Babylon was not merely a city on the Euphrates, but also a personification of human society, when it rises in pride against God and His will. But such a personification both with him and with other prophets,

including John in the Revelation, was possible only because of
the story in Gen. 11, which stamped an indelible character on
the city.

In exactly the same way the Flood lies as a dreadful
memory behind the Old Testament. Outside Genesis it is
referred to by its proper name (*mabul*) only in Psa. 29: 10,
which should be translated, 'Jehovah sat as king at the
Flood'. It is mentioned too as 'the waters of Noah' in Isa. 54: 9,
and possibly through the rainbow, if this is meant by 'the
faithful witness in the sky' (Psa. 89: 37). But it is only in the
light of the Flood and to a lesser extent the destruction of the
cities of the Plain that we can explain the unquestioned
acceptance of a universal judgment to come in the Day of
Jehovah. The loyalty of God in His promise to Noah after the
Flood helps to explain why Moses can praise Canaan as a land
'which the Lord your God cares for', in contrast to Egypt,
which is left to the unchanging laws of nature (Deut.
11: 1012).

THE FALL OF MAN

The virtual silence of the Old Testament about the Flood
makes it easier for us to understand why the story of the Fall
seems to play virtually no part in the thinking of the Old
Testament.

Is this really the case? It is quite common in some circles to
hear speakers stressing the delight of the pious Israelite in
the good things of this earth, corn and wine and oil, fertility in
flocks and herds, and many sons and daughters. It is
suggested that this is Israel's lot, while the Christian has a
heavenly calling and heavenly values and riches. This is too
simple. Let Asaph speak for many an Old Testament saint,
when he said,

> 'Whom have I in heaven but Thee?
> And there is nothing upon earth that I desire
>   besides Thee' (Psa. 73: 25).

In our days of scientific agriculture, when we bring our food
from the ends of the earth with little thought of starving or
half-starving millions, it is all too easy to forget that the

failure of the soil is the basic judgment on man (Gen. 3: 17–19). At least for the spiritually minded in Israel, the joy of harvest was not the joy of possessing but the joy of being blessed. The bountiful harvest was the sign that Jehovah had been merciful to them and had accepted them. This link between the abundant harvest and God's salvation is brought out clearly in Psa. 65.

It is true, however, that Israel refused to learn the deeper lesson of Gen. 3. A few of its greatest sons grasped it in moments of spiritual anguish and insight. When David had his eyes opened to realize that he had done what he had never conceived possible, he confessed to God,

> 'Behold, I was brought forth in iniquity,
> and in sin did my mother conceive me' (Psa. 51:5).

Isaiah, after he had been given a vision of the sin-bearing Servant, could confess,

> 'We have all become like one who is unclean,
> and our righteous deeds are like a polluted
> garment' (64: 6).

but few there were who understood him. Even today, while Judaism is capable of a very deep sense of sins committed, it has no understanding of or place for original sin, of a state of sin in which all efforts at reform are unavailing. Why should this be?

The confession, 'God, be merciful to me a sinner!' (Lk. 18: 13), if made sincerely, is probably the rarest and hardest that man can make. We are always tempted to think that under other conditions and circumstances we would have acted otherwise, and that even now, if we are but given a chance, we may yet make good. As we shall see later the bringing home of this fact is the great purpose of the histories of the Old Testament. But even the complete failure of Israel was insufficient to teach men the lesson. It was not until they crucified the Lord of glory that it became possible for the ordinary man to grasp that in him dwelt no good thing. So the full force of Gen. 3 had to await the cross for its understanding.

For all that, while the saints of the Old Testament did not and could not reach a New Testament consciousness of sin, yet their readiness to recognize their sins must have come from some realization that they belonged to a fallen race.

The question has been often raised, why there is so little reaching out to life beyond the grave in the Old Testament. Many reasons have been given, most of them valid in part, but it is too often overlooked that the pious accepted death as the necessary and just result of human sin. Death was not something natural, or a gateway to something better, but the inevitable outcome of what man had done. Not until God had transformed man would death automatically vanish (Isa. 25: 6–8). So it was only as special needs and stresses arose that the Holy Spirit drew men out to a vision of life after death and continued communion with God.

There is no quotation of or reference to the 'Protevangelium' (Gen. 3: 15) elsewhere in the Old Testament, but without it the prophetic promises of the Messianic king would have been impossible, for they would have been incomprehensible. The full reality could not really be foreseen until He came, but the longing for God's king and saviour remained an abiding power.

All could not have been foretold, for it would not have been understood. We may even question how far Isaiah fully grasped the implications of his Immanuel oracles (Isa. 7: 14–16; 8: 5–8; 9: 2–7; 11: 1–9). One of the reasons was the misunderstanding of the judgment on Eve (Gen. 3: 16), a misunderstanding which has lived on in the Church. Her love for her husband was to be turned to 'desire'. This is a rare word, found only three times, and its use in Gen. 4: 7 indicates something of the wild drive involved in it. Her husband would take advantage of it to rule over her. There is nothing in the Hebrew to suggest either a command or something seemly in a woman's being ruled by her husband. The ruling in place of partnership is a sign of the Fall. Hence men did not understand from Isa. 7: 14, and still less from Gen. 3: 15, that God would accomplish His purpose by using a despised woman alone.

CREATION AND PARADISE

Though the language of Gen. 1 is reflected in many of the psalms as well as in the prophets, it is clear that it took a very long time before the ordinary man was able to assimilate it both by faith and intellect. Until the Babylonian exile it was only the spiritual elite that could conceive of God as throned above His universe in solitary splendour, served by His angelic hosts. Further they could not go, for while some Christians, rightly or wrongly, have discovered in the light of the New Testament fore-shadowings of the Trinity in the Old, this is essentially a truth which we deduce from the teaching and nature of our Lord, and none of the saints in the Old Testament could be blamed for not deducing it from the revelation then given them.

For them it was hard enough to grasp that there could be a God who was not in some way tied to and influenced by His creation. The gods of the heathen were all part of the universe they controlled, and so in the last analysis they were also controlled by it. But Jehovah revealed Himself as the controller of all and uncontrolled by any. The idolatry that meets us repeatedly on the pages of the Old Testament was not an abandoning of the worship of Jehovah in favour of other gods, but a bringing of Jehovah into His creation and so subordinating Him to its control. Such a God would, of course, need the aid of other deities, who could then quite properly be honoured beside Him. It needed the Babylonian exile and the return to Palestine to burn these ideas out of Israel.

Then, however, the idea grew up among many of them, an idea that is not unknown in the Church, that there were angelic powers either not under God's control or only partially so. It needed the incarnation of the Son of God to demonstrate that the powers of evil, little though they may know it, and little though they may wish it, are accomplishing the purposes of God. This is one of the main themes of the Revelation of John.

It is perhaps unfortunate that many of us have become obsessed with the relationship of Gen. 1 to the discoveries of modern science. It has hindered us from realizing the true nature of the chapter and to what extent its language and concepts have left their mark on subsequent Scripture.

Sometimes we see it in the language of Hebrew poetry. Gen. 1: 2, which for many is merely a basis for discussion whether there was or was not a recreation in the world's history, has expressed itself repeatedly in the psalms and some of the prophets, especially Isaiah, in poetic imagery. We see God triumphing over the wild creatures of chaos, Leviathan and Rahab and the dragon in the waters. We see Him repeatedly as the ruler and controller of the sea which for the Israelite served as a picture of chaos, for man knew not how to make it submit to his laws.

One more example must suffice. In Dan. 7 we have a vision in which 'one like a son of man' is given the rule and dominion in the place of four beasts. The beasts are obviously four nations, but they are four nations as symbolized and expressed by four kings (v. 17). It has been claimed that the 'one like a son of man' is also a nation. So he is, for he is 'the saints of the Most High' *but only* as they are expressed and summed up in their King.

The true people of God are shown in their ruler as a man, the kingdoms of the earth are shown as beasts. This is far from being merely a condemnation of their character. The animals were made before man, that they might be ruled by man. Even so the natural beastlike kingdoms are first revealed in the vision, for it is their function, in so far as they are not destroyed, to be ruled by 'one like a son of man', who appears after them, although He has been from all eternity, and His people were chosen in Him before the foundation of the world. The fact that none of this needed explaining shows to what extent the language of the creation story had penetrated the thinking of Israel, though it may be but seldom directly referred to.

The subtlety of the outlook that lay behind so much of Israel's idolatry may be recognized in the concept of the Torah (the Mosaic law) in much of orthodox Judaism. Though the Torah is God's creation, it is often regarded as in some way binding or limiting Him in His actions. The same kind of thing may be found among Christian theologians, both crude and subtle, when they try to explain the death of Jesus Christ on the cross, by saying that God had to satisfy the demands of justice, of righteousness, or of the Law, as though these were eternal realities existing apart from God and in some way tying His hands. God is limited only by His own nature.

THREE

The Patriarchs

THE OPENING CHAPTERS OF GENESIS, AS HAS ALREADY BEEN pointed out, are concerned with the great facts that underlie the whole Biblical revelation. The personality of those who appear in them had little or no bearing on what happened, and they are not described. Suddenly with ch. 12 all is changed. We are introduced to a series of men and women whom we feel we would recognize if we were to meet them in daily life.

When, however, we study the stories more closely, we find that things are not as simple as they seem. Frequently made attempts to write biographies of the patriarchs show how little we are really told about them and for the most part they are filled out with second-rate fiction and archaeological snippets. Then too, when we turn to the archaeologist, he throws more light on the background of the patriarchal period than on any other part of the Old Testament, but the information seldom helps us to understand the stories better. On the contrary, it is my experience that many students find it hard to bring the archaeological facts to life, and repeatedly they are misunderstood and misused by most who are not experts.

In one way there is a striking similarity between these chapters and the story of creation in Gen. 1: 1–2:. Both have been so simplified that they appeal to all ages, cultures and intellects. Everything has been omitted that might distract us from the revelation these stories are meant to bring us. They are stories which deal with men's relationship with God, and all else is allowed to fall. This way of writing history is now generally called 'salvation history',[1] because it is intended to introduce us to the way God worked out men's salvation.

In the Upper Room Christ said to His Father, speaking of His disciples, 'I do not pray that Thou shouldst take them out of the world ... They are not of the world' (Jn. 17: 15, 16). This fact of being in but not of was no new revelation but merely a making explicit of what is implicit throughout the Old Testament. For the careful reader this is made clear in the stories about the patriarchs.

THE BACKGROUND OF GEN. 12–50

It is very easy so to read the stories as to picture the patriarchs moving about in an almost empty land, and so we have to be reminded that 'at that time the Canaanites and the Perizzites dwelt in the land' (Gen. 13: 7, also Gen. 12: 6). They were merely tolerated aliens who had to conform to the demands of those among whom they moved. Then the archaeologists have revealed to us that the period was one of major national movements, during which new nations appeared in the Fertile Crescent, as the arc of fertile ground between mountain and desert, and sea and desert, from the Persian Gulf through Iraq and Syria to the Egyptian frontier, is generally called today. Their final result was the conquest of Egypt by the Hyksos. But only in Gen. 14: 1–16 do these movements leave the least trace on the pages of Scripture, and then only to provide the background for the story of Abram and Melchizedek. These national movements doubtless co-operated blindly in the working out of God's purposes, but in themselves they are no part of salvation history and so find no mention.

Similarly we now know that the Hebrews were the same as the Habiru, to whom we have been introduced in Babylonian and Assyrian tablets and Egyptian inscriptions. W. F. Albright had argued convincingly that the Habiru or Hebrews were originally donkey caravaneers, and that that

[1] German 'Heilsgeschichte'.

is the meaning of Abram the Hebrew in Gen. 14: 13.[2] This would, in fact, explain how he could draw suddenly on 318 trained men (Gen. 14: 14). They would be mostly his donkey drivers. During the expedition of the four kings the caravan business would have to come to a stop, and Abraham would have called his men to headquarters at Hebron. There are no grounds for doubting that archaeology may throw similar light on the other patriarchs, but if it does we are not likely to understand and know them better, just as the fact of Abraham's being a caravaneer seems almost an irrelevance compared to the lessons to be learnt from the stories about him in the Bible. We should note, however, that unlike the later camel caravaneer, the donkey-man was only a semi-nomad, living on the fringe of settled society without becoming part of it.

Men must live in and as a part of society, but also and primarily they should live in relationship to God. So, before we are introduced to Israel, the society of God's creating, we are given the picture of their fathers in their relationship to God, a relationship that should have been shown by the Israelites as well, even as it must be by us. Hence the patriarchs' historical relationship to other men is as far as possible obliterated, so that it may not hinder our understanding of the spiritual side.

Another way of expressing this is to say that the patriarchs are types of men of faith, all that has no bearing on this typology being either suppressed or banished to a virtual appendix, e.g. Gen. 25: 1–6. (There is no compelling reason for looking on these verses as being in their strict chronological position. The children of Keturah were never intended to be the children of promise, as Sarah had once hoped to obtain a son through Hagar. Hence, though they have a place in Scripture, they are not allowed to interrupt the story of faith.)

We need no further confirmation than Heb. 11 that the patriarchs are heroes of faith, but we tend to forget it because we insist on reading into the stories another, incompatible typology as well. Abraham is made out to be a type of God the Father, both Isaac and Joseph of God the Son, Abraham's head servant – he was not Eliezar of Damascus! – of God the Holy Spirit. However attractive the resultant exegesis, it

[2] See especially his *The Biblical Period: From Abraham to Ezra.*

breaks down, because it cannot be applied to the stories consistently or to many of the details. Those responsible for the mistaken exegesis seem to have forgotten the great principle of spiritual analogy. Just as all true Christians since Christ have in varying measure shown Him forth in their lives, so all men of God before Him have prefigured Him in some measure, and this is at times particularly true of the patriarchs. But however much we lovingly draw out the analogies, we have no right to exalt them to God-created types.[3]

It would need a book to expound all the lessons on faith brought us in these chapters. Here we must content ourselves with the outstanding lessons from the four main characters.

ABRAHAM

It appears as though we were intended to see faith virtually in the abstract in Abraham's life. Quite startlingly we are told nothing of his antecedents and background. We owe to Joshua (Jos. 24: 2) our knowledge that he was brought up in a polytheistic family. Incidentally we must not make Sir Leonard Woolley's assumption that Abraham was in any sense a citizen of Ur. If he was a donkey caravaneer, he may have had as little real link with that Sumerian city as he later had with Hebron or Beer-sheba. We are told nothing of how he came to faith, for, little though some realize it, it is not how we come to faith, but how we walk the path of faith, that really matters.

Abraham's faith showed itself in three particular directions. First there was obedience, 'He went out not knowing where he was to go' (Heb. 11: 8). We should beware of exaggeration. If his main livelihood was with caravans, then a look at a map of the Ancient Near East will show us that the general direction of his move must have been clear enough to him. What remained unknown was where the end of his trek might be. There is no suggestion that he was called to something entirely alien to him; we do not find this until we reach Joseph.

Then there was trust in God's keeping power. The whole

3 See Appendix I.

civilization from the Persian Gulf to the frontier of Egypt was based on fortified settlements, rather grandiloquently called 'cities' in the English translations. Miss Kenyon's excavations at Jericho suggest that its town wall dates back to c.7000 B.C., though the settlement may be another thousand years older! In other words, the whole tradition of the Fertile Crescent took human methods of protection based on the 'city' for granted. Abraham, however, was prepared to live in tents out in the open country, depending entirely on God for safety both from wild men and wild beasts (Heb. 11:9).

The third element in his faith was his willingness to believe in God's future purpose. In due course the steady onward march reached its goal; the trusting tent-dweller came to know by experience God's wall around him. But Abraham had to go down to his grave in Machpelah's cave still trusting that one day the promises would be fulfilled. Isaac's birth had shown that they could be, and his receiving him back from the grave, figuratively speaking (Heb. 11: 19), confirmed that he was the seed of promise. But for all that he was laid to rest with his eyes still looking for the dawning of fulfilment.

It is worth noting the main weakness of Abraham's faith. We are not told why he broke his journey in Haran (Gen. 11: 31; Acts 7: 4), and in the absence of knowledge we do well not to guess and still less to criticize. He doubted God's protection in Egypt (Gen. 12: 10–20) and among the Philistines (Gen. 20). In some measure he doubted God's promises when he took Hagar as Sarah's child-bearing substitute (Gen. 16: 1–4). The whole area of civilization from Sumeria to Canaan was governed by laws, which, however much they varied in detail, expressed a similar outlook on life. It was a unitary civilization, just as is Europe today west of the iron curtain. Similarly the religions had much in common. But Egypt, in civilization, culture and religion, had gone its own path. Similarly, whatever the origin of the Philistines, they were aliens to Canaan and its civilization. In other words, Abraham was not the first to hesitate when faced by the completely strange. Then too what Sarah asked of her husband, when she offered him Hagar as her child-bearer, was part and parcel of the tradition in which Abraham had grown up, cf. Gen. 30: 1–3, 9. The faith that hesitates before the completely alien is in danger of swimming with the stream in the normal courses of life.

ISAAC

There are two outstanding features in Isaac's life. One is that he was prepared to be a sacrificial victim. The young man who could carry enough wood up the hill for a burnt offering could clearly have evaded the efforts of a man of 120 or over to sacrifice him. A careful reading of Gen. 22 compels us to believe that Isaac was as prepared to be sacrificed as Abraham was to sacrifice him.

The other was that he was prepared to continue his father's manner of life. This should not be looked on as obvious. Gen. 24: 10, 22–27 makes it clear that Rebekah lived in Haran or a nearby town. She may well have urged her husband to seek a secure home, but if she did, he refused, though it seems clear that he suspended his custom for a time in Gerar; he may only have pitched his tents within the town walls (Gen. 26: 6–8), without moving into a house.

His great failure was one that men of faith are always prone to, the belief that he had come to a full knowledge of God's will. Though the oracle to Rebekah (Gen. 25: 23), which was surely known to Isaac, is unambiguous, Isaac allowed himself to be influenced by Esau's bodily build and strength and so convinced himself that it must be he who was to receive the blessing. God had acted even-handedly and fairly. If Jacob was to receive the blessing, Esau was entitled to the birthright. By Isaac's refusal to accept God's foretelling he lost Esau both blessing and birthright.

JACOB

We are too ready to judge Jacob by the biased opinion of his brother (Gen. 27: 36). Whatever Esau might think, he had no claim to the blessing, and he had sold his birthright for what at the time had seemed to him a fair price. Indeed, we probably exaggerate his language for it is very doubtful whether Jacob means 'supplanter'. 'Overreacher' seems a more suitable rendering. If we are willing to use modern colloquialisms, we could render the verse, 'Is he not rightly named Smart Dealer, for he has outsmarted me these two times?'

However much we dislike him, Jacob is presented as essentially a man of faith. He knows and values what God has promised him, but instead of allowing God to keep His promise in His own way he uses every method, fair or foul, to obtain what he believes is his. That is why there is nowhere even a whisper of condemnation of the part played by Rebekah and Jacob. They had to deal with an obstinate old man, who had argued himself into the conviction that he was doing God's will. When he grasped that God's will had in fact been done against all his own efforts, he collapsed like a punctured balloon (Gen. 27: 33) and hardened his heart against Esau's pleas – note RV,mg, RSV rendering of Gen. 27: 39.

There is no evidence that Jacob ever wavered in his faith in God's promises, but it was not until his wrestling with 'God' that he learnt that the God who promised also had his ways of fulfilling what he had promised. It is a pity that AV misinterprets the new name Israel. Beyond doubt it must be interpreted as 'He who strives with God', or 'God strives'. The second is preferable, for it implicitly includes the former, and it stresses that God had chosen Jacob and would not release him until He had accomplished His purposes. Jacob is not an attractive character, but then the man who is trying to do God's will by his own strength and wisdom never is. His own verdict was, 'Few and evil have been the days of the years of my life' (Gen. 47: 9).

JOSEPH

Joseph is the Old Testament foreshadowing of and counterpart to Rom. 8: 28, 'We know that in everything God works for good with those who love Him'. Paul can affirm 'We know', but many Christians find it very hard to believe. Nowhere more than in Joseph's life, if we look away from our Lord Himself, do we find this truth demonstrated. Joseph understood this himself. He said to his brothers, 'Do not be distressed, or angry with yourselves, because you sold me here; for God sent me before you to preserve life . . . So it was not you who sent me here, but God' (Gen. 45: 5, 8). He expressed it even more pointedly after his father's death, 'As for you, you meant evil against me; but God meant it for good, to bring it about that many people should be kept alive, as they are today' (Gen. 50: 20).

There are other features about Joseph that call for brief notice. We have come to take it almost for granted, when we find him promoted as overseer of Potiphar's house. We overlook that this involved not only a perfect knowledge of Egyptian, but also the ability to read and write in Egyptian. This was a difficult thing to do and the opportunity to learn was given to few; it must have been through God's intervention, but when God intervened the slave took his opportunity. One of the more important aspects of faith is the willingness to see God's will in the opportunities He offers us.

Some picture Joseph, the prime minister of Egypt and the confidant of Pharaoh, going down to the main grain-store and selling wheat to all who might come. The very idea is ridiculous. True enough, he must have toured the stores to see that his subordinates were doing their duty and not enriching themselves from the need of others, but it was not chance that he was in the right place at the right time. No foreigners were allowed over the frontier without reference to the capital, and we may be sure that Joseph scanned the list of applicants daily. So his inspection brought him to the right place at the right time. But why had Joseph not discovered the whereabouts of his father long before? After all, all the resources of the Egyptian secret service were at his disposal. We must assume that Joseph knew that he could not know without acting, and premature action would probably have meant the break up of his family, for Jacob's anger could be very terrible. He was willing to await the time of God's choice for the family reunion, for after all he had God's promise it would come; God had given him his two dreams to that effect when he was still a lad.

Let us finally note that Joseph had riches and honour and power such as very few men of God attain to, and they remained with him to the very end. He did not experience the proverbial ingratitude of princes. For all that he never regarded them as an end in themselves, nor did he look on Egypt as his home. He knew that he had been an instrument in the working out of God's plans, which should ripen in another age and in another country, and he wished that at least his bones should share in the fulfilment (Gen. 50: 24, 25).

We should be prepared to accept the fact that the New Testament does not refer to Joseph except casually in connection with his last request (Heb. 11: 22), and that it nowhere suggests that he was a type of Jesus Christ. As one of the choicest saints of the Old Testament he foreshadowed Him in many a point, but that is another matter.[4]

[4] See Appendix I.

FOUR

The Story of Redemption

BY IMMEMORIAL CUSTOM, BOTH JEWISH AND CHRISTIAN, THE FIVE books of Moses have been called the Law of Moses, or simply the Law. The name is not strictly accurate, for, as we have seen, Gen. 1–11 provide an introduction to revelation generally and Gen. 12–50 to the history of Israel in particular. The term, the Law, is strictly applicable only to Exodus to Deuteronomy. Even here there is need for qualification. In the edition of my study bible, in these four books 165 columns are taken up by law, 44 by exhortation and 109 by history. The count is perforce somewhat rough and ready, but it is sufficiently accurate to prove the point. As we understand the term 'law', Exodus to Deuteronomy are far from being simply a law code.

The Hebrew word, which we render 'law', is *torah*, and this means teaching or instruction. True enough, God's instruction has the force of law, but we obtain a false emphasis, if we so translate. The Septuagint, the standard Greek translation of the Old Testament in the time of Christ, translated *torah* by *nomos*, which in its New Testament use we normally render 'law'. Though *nomos* can mean statute law, it means fundamentally usage or custom, and then a norm or principle. So our translations, especially the older ones, very often give a wrong slant to Paul's arguments.

Once we remember that *torah* means instruction, we can see the appropriateness of the name not merely to the four books that deal with the work of Moses but also to all five books of the Pentateuch, for the history given in them is intended for our learning just as much as the laws and exhortation.

THE GOD WHO ACTS

In the two previous chapters I stressed how selective was the
information given us both in the Primaeval Revelation and in
the stories about the Patriarchs, and I used the term
'salvation history' for the principle that lies behind this
selectivity. Those details were chosen by the Holy Spirit
which most clearly showed God's working out of man's
salvation and man's reaction to it. This principle is continued
in the history of the Exodus and wanderings in the wilderness. This explains why the typology of the New Testament is
drawn almost entirely, though not quite, from the Pentateuch. It is true that very much in the later history of Israel
can correctly be called salvation history, but it seldom bears
that stamp of universality we find at the beginning.

Passages like Hos. 2: 1–9: 10; Jer. 2: 2, 3; Ezek. 16: 8–14
sound strange to the superficial reader of the Pentateuch, as
do indeed the blessings pronounced by Balaam, cf. especially
Num. 23: 21. They make sense only for those who remember
that the story in the way it is told us in the Bible is highly
selective. If it had been told us by a modern romantic author,
we should have been reminded of the superhuman difficulties
that lay in the way of Israel. The weariness of the way would
have been graphically pictured, and the difficulties of
learning the way of the desert described. This side did exist,
and the Bible indicates that it knows it existed. But the
purpose of the story is to glorify God's strength and triumph.
Modern man loves to stress the glorious failure in which man
is praiseworthy even in failure. Salvation history knows man
merely as inglorious failure and God as conqueror.

The opening of the Exodus story introduces us to a principle
we later find repeatedly in revelation, viz. 'in the fulness of
time'. God did not intervene in salvation until Israel was
desperate. We are repeatedly moved to ask why God should
be, humanly speaking, so slow in acting. The answer is not, as
is so often suggested, that God's time-scale is not ours, though
this is true enough. It is that He must always first bring man
to an end of himself and his hopes.

Then we have the principle that God reveals Himself both
in act and word through men of His choice and preparation.
Here again we see the difference in the modern fictional
biographies of Moses. In them all the local factors in Egypt

and Midian that will have influenced him are lovingly described and evaluated. Not so in the Bible. It knows full well that these factors accomplished nothing except as they were used by God, and so they are passed over in almost complete silence. It is the end-product, as trained by God, that matters. Similarly in the New Testament we are told virtually nothing of the silent years in Nazareth.

The third principle that emerges is less easy to express simply. God is not merely the Creator but also the Sustainer of this world. The orderly state of nature as we know it is due to God's action, but it is an action which makes it possible for the scientist to tabulate 'the laws of nature'. Normally it is under such conditions that God speaks to men and leads them. His miracles for them come less from His changing their circumstances, and more from His leading them into such circumstances as will work for their good. But in the decisive moments of human redemption God breaks into nature. There is very little in the stories of the Patriarchs that the onlooker would have called miraculous. Now in Egypt all suddenly glows with the miraculous. From the hardening of Pharaoh's heart on (Ex. 4: 21) the movement of natural forces become geared to the working out of God's will, and the generation of the Exodus becomes the instrument by which God reveals His principles of redemption and salvation.

THE TYPOLOGY OF THE HISTORY OF REDEMPTION

Man ate of the tree of knowledge and from then on he has been consumed by the thirst to know. Thanks to the writings of Manetho, an Egyptian priest (*c.* 250 B.C.), which have come down to us in the works of those who quoted him, much was known of Egyptian history even before the decipherment of Egyptian hieroglyphic writing in the middle of last century. Hence from at least the time of Josephus (1st cent. A.D.) efforts have been made to fix the time and the identity of the Pharaoh of the Exodus.

Not so was salvation history written. When God acted, He was dependent neither on circumstances or human agents, for a Moses could have been raised up at another time. Hence the date is not given and the king of Egypt becomes a mere anonymous actor. In spite of belief to the contrary, neither the route of the Exodus nor the actual site of Sinai-Horeb are known with certainty. That is why the whole story can be used typologically, for in its essence it is not tied to the accidents of time and space.

This does not apply to the fulfilment of the type. Though the Exodus is one of the shadows of good things to come, God's shadows have more reality than man's most concrete facts. The eternal and vital reality of the Exodus came from the life, death and resurrection of Jesus Christ. It did not matter at what point in history the shadow might begin. The calculations that used to be made to show, that it was at some mathematically important date in human history have been shown by archaeology to be valueless. But when we come to the basic fact of our redemption, we are allowed to place it with certainty in its setting in world history (Luke 3: 1, 2).

There is one point in the Egyptian background of redemption that merits mention. As Moses indicated indirectly in Deut. 11: 10–12, Egypt was the land known to the Old Testament where the greatest uniformity of nature ruled. Except for irregularities in the rise and fall of the Nile in flood time, its inhabitants could foretell the next day, the next week, the next month with reasonable certainty. It is not so difficult for men to believe in the existence of God and to pray to Him – I do not say *trust* Him – in the midst of catastrophe, for there is nothing else left to do. It is amidst the predictable uniformities of life that faith withers away and religion becomes formalistic. All the plagues, except of course the last, showed God's rule and triumph just in these uniformities. It was only after this that God divided the Red Sea, or Sea of Reeds. Throughout the Bible the sea stands as a picture of chaos, of that which does not conform to law and order. Thus God is seen as the ruler of the law-bound and the lawless alike.

ISRAEL'S FAILURE

From one point of view Israel was bound to fail. Part of God's purpose in Israel was to demonstrate the completeness of the Fall of man, that he would continue to fall even under the most favourable of circumstances. Since at Sinai God gave a *torah*, but not the power to keep it, the history of Israel could not fail to display man's falling short of God's glory. But there were certain specific reasons for failure as well.

The Exodus meant a new beginning, which was confirmed by the covenant at Sinai. But the bulk of the people continued to live in the past. There was the continual hankering after Egypt. The supernatural gives its thrill for the moment, but then we look back with longing for the natural. Some of the passages are Ex. 16: 3; Num. 11: 4, 5; 14: 2–4; 20: 5; 21: 5. The last two are especially instructive, for they come from a time when very few of the Israelites had any living memory of Egypt. Most who had grown up there had already died.

Far more important is the incident of the golden bull – the rendering 'calf' is both erroneous and foolish. Joshua, in taking farewell of the people, reveals unexpectedly that the gods of Mesopotamia still played a living part in the lives of the Israelites so many centuries later (Jos. 24: 2, 14). The golden bull made by Aaron is the most interesting example of this.

The suggestion is often met that it was made under the influence of the Egyptian Apis bull worship. The people's words, 'These are your gods, (or, 'This is your god'), O Israel, who brought you up out of the land of Egypt' (Ex: 32: 4), should in themselves have been sufficient disproof of this nonsense. They were not suggesting that Egypt's gods had turned against their own country. We know that the bull was one of the oldest and commonest of the symbols used by the Semites for deity. It is a commonplace even today to find that devout and orthodox Christians hold concepts which have come down from pre-reformation days and sometimes from an even earlier pagan past. Israel had not realized the truth contained in Paul's words, 'If any one is in Christ, he is a new creation' (2 Cor. 5: 17).

Along with the living in the past went the unpreparedness for the new present. As we read of the continued fears, grumbles and lack of faith, we may well be tempted to sympathize and to think that we might have done the same. If we do so, it is because we all too often act as they did.

We may look on it as natural that we should be afraid and doubtful, when we find ourselves in completely unfamiliar and threatening circumstances. The sin in Eden consisted in Eve's and Adam's thinking that they were capable of facing an unknown future without God, provided that they had sufficient knowledge. Man's fear of the unknown is his recognition that his parents were wrong. For those who profess that they have reversed the sin of Eden by becoming God's people to fear the novel and difficult shows that their profession is at the best incomplete.

THE GRACE OF COVENANT

The original edition of the 'Schofield Bible' in its note on Gen. 12: 1 has the amazing statement, 'The Dispensation of Promise ended when Israel rashly accepted the law', and this is implied in more cautious language in the note on Ex. 19: 3.

In the past there has been a tendency to regard a covenant as an agreement or bargain between two parties. It is now known from the work of the archaeologist that this is true only when the covenant was between *equals*. Between the superior and the inferior, and above all between God and man, after a recitation of the superior's acts a gracious promise is made, conditional on his will being accepted. This is what we find in Ex. 19: 3–6.

First we have a recitation of God's gracious acts, then the offer of a position of privilege, an offer which went far beyond anything said to the Patriarchs. The terms of the covenant are not given because they had to be accepted in pure faith in the gracious character of the covenant-making God. The people accepted God's offer in sheer faith (Ex. 19: 8). The suggestion that Moses and the people were acting against their best interests and contrary to the highest will of God seems to be a strange hallucination. The giving of the Law was a necessary stage in God's revelation of Himself to men and an inescapable step on the way towards the Redeemer's coming. No higher privilege could have been offered Israel. We should do well to remember Moses' praise of the Law (Deut. 4: 8), and God's commendation of the people's action (Deut. 5: 28, 29).

There is another point we should not overlook. Human logic has linked election and reprobation or rejection. It is assumed that because He has elected some that therefore the others are left to their own devices, which means ultimate condemnation, or that God has even ruled that they must be lost. In Ex. 19: 5 the very affirmation of the choice of Israel as

God's own possession is linked with the statement that the whole earth is His.[1] However wonderful the truth of election, it must never be so formulated as to imply that some are damned because they have no possibility of salvation.

The nature of the covenant requirements must be left to the next chapter. For the moment we must content ourselves with noting that hardly had the covenant been made than it was broken by the people by the making of a golden bull.

Presumably because it could be argued that those who came out of Egypt had been so steeped in the paganism of their surroundings there that they could not do otherwise than break the covenant, the covenant was renewed before Moses' death (Deut. 29: 1), only to be broken by Achan's sin. It was renewed again by Joshua before his death (Jos. 24: 25). There is every reason for thinking that scholars are correct in assuming that covenant-renewal ceremonies were a regular part of Israel's worship. But every renewal – who gave them authority to renew that which had been made by God? – was followed only by fresh sin and decline. The remaining story of the Old Testament is one of grace amid sin.

Jeremiah in proclaiming the New Covenant had to say, 'Behold, the days are coming, says the LORD, when I will make a new covenant with the house of Israel and the house of Judah, not like the covenant which I made with their fathers when I took them by the hand to bring them out of the land of Egypt, forasmuch as they broke My covenant, and I had to lord it over them, says the LORD' (Jer. 31: 31, 32). This is the true translation of the Hebrew, as is recognized both by the Septuagint and by many Continental translations. The history of Israel in the Old Testament reveals what it means when God's people do not do His will. He does not cast them off, but they experience the gracious handling of the Master and Lord and not the fellowship of the heavenly Father. Much the same could be said today of many a local church and of many an individual Christian.

---

[1] In addition the word *'am* (people), normally confined to Israel is used of the nations of the world in general, while Israel is called a holy nation (*goi*), though *goi* is the normal term for the nations at large.

FIVE

The Law

IN THE PREVIOUS CHAPTER WE SAW THAT TO TRANSLATE *torah*, AND
even the New Testament *nomos*, by law is misleading. In
itself *torah* means primarily 'instruction'. This word of
caution is strongly reinforced, when we turn to the Pentateuch to study 'the Law of Moses'. If we use the term strictly,
we find that it does not exist in the Bible.

For the sake of brevity and convenience we may ignore a
few isolated commandments. Apart from them there are
three larger and one smaller collections of commandments
and ordinances concerned mainly with daily life; in addition
there are several large groups of laws and regulations dealing
with the people's worship. We shall find also that the former
are divided into two quite dissimilar groups of laws, which by
scholars have been called by the rather grandiloquent names
of 'casuistic' and 'apodeictic'.

The law of Moses which we meet so often in the New
Testament is really the result of centuries of work begun by
Ezra – for all we know the process could have begun even
earlier and continued down to the completion of the Talmud
about A.D. 550. Indeed one could say in one sense that the
work has continued down to our day. It was as natural for
Jews to construct a law-code on the basis of the indications
given in the Pentateuch as it was for Christians to devise
systematic theologies from theological statements in the
Bible; both efforts refused to recognize that God could have
done the work far better Himself, if that had been His
purpose.

THE BASIC LAW

The original law given to Israel was very far from what later generations conceived it to be. In the last chapter we saw that Israel accepted God's terms for the covenant even before it knew what they were to be (Ex. 19: 3–8). Three days later God spoke the words of the Ten Commandments to *all* the people (Ex. 20: 1–17); these and these only were spoken directly by God, all the rest being mediated by Moses. Quite apart from anything else this would make us assume that the Ten Commandments occupy a peculiar and special position in the making known of God's will.

The Book of the Covenant (for the term see Ex. 24: 7) which followed the Ten Commandments (Ex. 20: 22–23: 33) was given to Moses to communicate to Israel (Ex. 20: 19, 22), who accepted it (Ex. 24: 7). Then the covenant was solemnly made.

Let us be quite clear that God did not get His people at a disadvantage and force them to accept commandment after commandment once they had expressed their willingness to do His will. If we understand the Ten Commandments and the Book of the Covenant aright, they contain all that God was demanding of His people, if it was to be in covenant relationship to Him. If we meditate on the Book of the Covenant, both on what it says and what it leaves unsaid, we shall surely come to the conclusion that it is little more than an explanatory commentary on how the Ten Commandments were to be carried out. This can be expressed by saying that the Ten Commandments contain a statement of the great basic principles of character which must exist if a man wishes to be in fellowship with God; all the rest is commentary and a guide towards the creation of this character.

This is expressed symbolically by the placing of the two tables of stone, but not the Book of the Covenant, inside the Ark. The Ark itself was covered by the mercy-seat or *kapporet*. The wings of the cherubim, stretched out horizontally over the mercy-seat, symbolized the throne of God in the midst of His people. If He was conceived of as occupying His throne, then His feet would rest on the mercy-seat, and the tables of the law would so be protected. The principles were immutable; the commentary would or should vary from

generation to generation. A detailed study of the Book of the
Covenant should convince us that it was intended for people
living in a fairly primitive agricultural society. That is why
the prophets so seldom gratify ritualists by attacking
breaches of the ceremonial law with which the Ten Commandments are not concerned.

THE OTHER CODES

How then are we to understand the nature and purpose of the
other three codes of law concerned with daily life?

That in Ex. 34: 10–28 is so brief that for our purposes we
can ignore it. There seems to be no discernible purpose in its
choice of commandments. All that can be said is that all,
except v. 13, repeat directly or by implication laws already
given. We find v. 13 in Deut. 7: 5; 12: 3, but the sin with the
golden bull is enough explanation for the development here.

The next code chronologically[1] is the Law of Holiness (Lev.
17–26) – so called by modern scholars because of the frequent
repetition of 'You shall be holy, for I am holy, says the LORD'.
Then at the close of the wilderness period we have the Law of
Deuteronomy (Deut. 5; 12–30) which also puts the Ten
Commandments in pride of place.

If we undertake the rewarding but somewhat tiring task of
comparing the Book of the Covenant, the Law of Holiness and
the Law of Deuteronomy with one another, we shall first of all
discover that there is a difference in kind among them. The
Book of the Covenant is for the most part pure law (the main
exception is mentioned later). True enough, it is not
expressed in the circumlocutions of modern statute law, but it
is normally law such as a modern lawyer can appreciate and
which he could easily rewrite in modern terms. Obviously we
must except the blessings and curses which form part of all
these codes, cf. Ex. 23: 20–33. In the Law of Holiness we gain
the impression that we are being told God's will against the
aweful background of the revelation of God's holiness in the
Tabernacle. It is no longer pure law but rather a reflection of

[1] We are concerned here with the order of the Pentateuch, not with
the suggestions of some scholars.

God's holiness in His people. In Deuteronomy the most characteristic expression is, perhaps, 'You are the sons of the Lord your God; you shall not . . .' (Deut. 14: 1). The legal section of the book is almost more a practical sermon to those who have had a deep experience of God than a repetition of the Law, as its misleading name, taken from the Greek, might lead us to believe. This is something few will challenge unless they are committed to the rabbinic system of dealing with the revelation to Moses. In other words, the educational purpose of the *torah* lies clearly on its pages.

Educationally, then, the existence of three law codes should not surprise us. When we look at the laws, however, which make them up, we meet the entirely unexpected. Quite a fair number are found in one code and one code only, while very few are found in all three. What is more, it would be quite impossible to arrange the commandments in order of importance by appealing to the number of times each is found. More curious still is that the Book of the Covenant makes no claims to completeness. It omits matters, e.g. laws concerning marriage, for which legislation must have existed.

CASUISTIC AND APODEICTIC LAW

The earlier mentioned division into Casuistic and Apodeictic law may help us to understand these problems better. As already said, most of the laws are essentially of a type which the modern lawyer would recognize, though he would not always agree that they should be brought into a legal code. There are, especially in Deuteronomy, certain do's and don'ts, mostly of a fairly elementary character, which spring from the fact that Israel is God's people, e.g. Deut. 22: 5–8. But on the whole the general pattern is one common to the early law codes of the ancient Near East. We are told that if a man does so and so, then the penalty shall be the following. Quite often the motivation or the circumstances of the action are mentioned and the penalty is fixed accordingly. These laws are now called casuistic laws by scholars because they deal with stated cases.

There are, however, other laws which are quite alien to normal civil law. If they do not startle us, it is merely because we are so familiar with them. They are demands to which no exceptions are made, and there is only one penalty in the case where it is mentioned. Their nature will be best understood, if the more important of them have their references given.

First and foremost there are the Ten Commandments. The continual discussion about how they are to be understood, especially the prohibitions of the second table, is sufficient to show that they cut across our normal modes of thinking. Then there are those offences where the penalty is 'shall be put to death' (RSV), 'shall surely be put to death' (AV), Hebrew *mut yamut*, e.g. Ex. 21: 12 (Lev. 24: 17); 21: 15, 16, 17 (Lev. 20: 9); 22: 18 (Lev. 20: 27), Lev. 20: 10, 12; 24: 16. Finally there is the series of solemn curses on certain actions in Deut. 27: 15–26.

This type of law, which the modern scholar calls apodeictic, was at the time peculiar to Israel and springs entirely from its relationship to God. Such absolute demands can only rarely be made by the community on an individual. So far as we can read between the lines of the Pentateuch Abraham brought with him from Mesopotamia a definite code of law and conduct, which though much simpler than codes like those of Hammurabi were very much of the same type. Israel in Egypt will for its own affairs have continued under this ancestral code.

At Sinai God faced His people with a series of absolute demands. So far as He was concerned, this was His will. However, man does not live to God alone but also in the relativities of human life and society. So it would seem that God took laws from Israel's tradition and redrafted them in the light of the basic Ten Commandments to show how they would have to remodel the whole of life. If this is so, there was no need for God to cover every aspect of life, as the rabbis later felt compelled to do. He was teaching them, and in the advance from the Book of the Covenant to the Law of Holiness, and from this to Deuteronomy we can trace some of the steps in the education. David was merely following in this pattern, when he made the law of 1 Sam. 30: 24. Its mention in Scripture is the Holy Spirit's endorsement that he had rightly learnt. This education was carried still further in the Sermon on the Mount. Our Lord took the same basic principles and applied them to the lives of those whose character conformed to the picture given in the Beatitudes.

THE CEREMONIAL LAW

In addition to the codes of law already studied there is much ceremonial law – it is not missing from these codes but plays a small part in them. The main sections of ceremonial law are Ex. 25–31, Lev. 1–16 and many chapters in Numbers.

The first thing we have to note is that no ceremonial law was given until after the covenant had been made. Obviously Israel must have had a sacrificial ritual alongside its civil law. Since the Bible does not tell us how it came into being or from where it came, we are entitled to make what guesses we think are edifying, but the edification is no proof that the guesses are true. God used the old for the making of the covenant and then gave something new. In all probability the new, just as with the civil law, was a remoulding of the old so that it might carry God's lesson.

If the sacrificial ritual and the Tabernacle were not given until after the covenant had been made, it means that the covenant did not rest on correct ritual, but that the ritual obtained its meaning and power from the covenant.

We may put this in another way by saying that the ceremonial law with its place of worship and sacrifices was given not to create the covenant but to maintain it once it had been made. An interesting confirmation of this is seen in the appointment of the Day of Atonement, not from the first, but when it had been made necessary by the sin of Aaron's two elder sons (Lev. 6: 1–3). The discerning evangelist has discovered long ago that, while he can preach the Cross very effectively on the basis of the Passover sacrifice, the message of the Levitical sacrifices seldom appeals except to the converted man, or to one who already intellectually knows the Christian message.

The Tabernacle, later the Temple, with its sacrifices was a spiritual reality, but the reality came through their being shadows of good things to come. The blood of bulls and of goats cannot take away sin; it can only speak of the eternal sacrifice of Christ, from which it draws its validity. The New Testament lays no stress on our Lord's conforming to the ceremonial law, though numerous hints show that He did. What does stand out is how He fulfilled the moral law, rising far above all criticism and condemnation.

Those who have experienced in their lives the reality

behind the ritual and the ceremonial will find themselves living as their Lord lived. They will keep the basic principles of the law, not because they feel themselves under obligation to do so, but because the life of Christ is being lived out in them. The Ten Commandments express in human words and situations God's moral character. In the measure that we fail to show their spiritual fulfilment we deny our claim to be sons of God.

SIX

The Former Prophets

AT THE END OF DEUTERONOMY WE FIND ISRAEL, THE PEOPLE OF God, at the highest level it was to reach in the Old Testament, however much prophetic voices might foretell infinitely higher attainment in the ages to come. Israel was standing on the brink of God's fulfilment of His promises to give them the land, and they already held Transjordan as an earnest of the fulfilment. All the corrupting links with Egypt had vanished during the forty years of wandering. The Law had been expounded in its deeper ethical significance. And so the covenant was renewed (Deut. 29: 1). At the same time the sin of Baal-peor (Num. 25) foreshadowed trouble to come – this is underlined in the Song of Moses (Deut. 31: 6–32: 47).

In the Hebrew Bible there follow the four books known as The Former Prophets, viz. Joshua, Judges (not Ruth!), Samuel, Kings. the two latter being each one book in the Hebrew MSS but not in the printed Bibles.[1] They are known as prophetic books, in contrast to our calling them historical, not because prophets appear in them or because they were written by prophets, even though they were indubitably written under prophetic guidance. God has two main ways by which He reveals Himself, by what He does and by what He says. The two can never be completely dissociated, but where the former predominates we have what we call history. Where the latter predominates we have prophecy, as we term it. But for the Bible both are prophecy, because both declare the character and will of God.

[1] See Appendix II.

THE DECLINE OF ISRAEL

Before we look at The Former Prophets as individual books we shall do well to consider the story unfolded in them as a whole. Almost at the beginning of Joshua we have the story of Achan, which in a very real sense corresponds in the history of Israel to the fall in Eden in the history of mankind. There can be little doubt that it was his sin that began the process of separation between his tribe, Judah, and the tribes that later called themselves Israel, a separation that was finally to destroy both Israel and Judah. We should probably see its shadow over Joshua's little regarded prophecy, 'You cannot serve the LORD; for He is a holy God; He is a jealous God; He will not forgive your transgressions or your sins' (Jos. 24: 19).

Once Joshua and his younger contemporaries were dead the history of Israel becomes the story of steady decline until there was no remedy left but exile. We devote most of our attention to the heroes of faith whom God raised up to stop the rot, and so we fail to realize that they seldom, if ever, raised the national level of life and religion. They were able to stop the Gadarene rush to destruction and to remove the worst of the outward signs of men's corrupt behaviour and religion, but there is all too much evidence that basically the people were little influenced.

Perhaps the greatest of these men of God was Samuel, yet, even while his physical powers were still unimpaired, the people came demanding a king. Because of our over-typological reading of the Old Testament many of us have never realized that neither king nor temple were God's intention for His people and that His giving of them meant His second best for them. It is not chance that there is a typology of the Tabernacle but not of the Temple. However much spiritual benefit may have come to Israel and to the Church through the two temples, Solomon's and Zerubbabel's, there were features about both of them that were bound to foster false concepts of religion.

Similarly, kingship unavoidably brought social deterioration with it. David was a man after God's own heart, but even in his reign those social troubles had begun which led to the disruption of the kingdom after Solomon's death and which were so unsparingly denounced by the great eighth and sixth century prophets. From our position of advantage after the events it is easy to see the weaknesses in David's rule, which were unconnected with his sin.

There is no evidence of any official attempt at religious reform in the North until it was far too late (2 Ki. 17: 2). In Judah there were a number of religious reformations which showed how far the people had fallen, but there is virtually no evidence for any attempt to tackle the social degeneration and injustice – the one exception is Jer. 26: 19, which has left no trace in the story in Kings. Just as the institution of the sanctuaries at Bethel and Dan with their bull images by Jeroboam the son of Nebat made religious reformation as good as impossible in the North, so the very institution of kingship made a cure for social evil virtually unobtainable, because it ran counter to the basis of Israelite society laid down in the Law.

It is not surprising then that God should in due time reject that which had shown itself unreformable. The doom on the North was announced to Elijah at Mt. Horeb, i.e. Sinai (1 Ki. 19: 15–17). Elijah told God, at least by implication, that the covenant had failed (1 Ki. 19: 14). The judgment pronounced by God showed that He accepted His prophet's verdict, but He promised that a remnant of 7,000 surely meaning the perfect number of God's choice would be saved. In God's grace the doom was deferred for about a century and a quarter, but the day came when Assyria destroyed Samaria and led the leaders of the people into exile. A little over a century after Elijah the same doom was pronounced over Judah (Isa. 6: 8–13). This also was deferred for a century and a half until Nebuchadnezzar destroyed Jerusalem and its temple. When Judah too went into exile, the history that began at the Exodus ended. It seemed to begin again in 538 B.C., when the Jews were permitted to return to Judea and Jerusalem. In practice, however, it never did. As we shall see in ch. 11 the Inter-Testamental Period was not a mere continuation of the past but the beginning of something new. The remnant that returned was not merely a truncated version of the past; it had no real political existence at all. It is no mere chance that we can assume with reasonable certainty that at all times from 538 B.C. onwards more Jews were living outside Palestine than in it. So the Former Prophets give us the history of the failure of Israel as a political institution.

JOSHUA

The book of Joshua is normally misunderstood because it is assumed to be a history of the conquest of Canaan. In fact the first twelve chapters primarily record the mighty acts of God during the Conquest. There is so much omitted that we cannot piece these stories together with absolute certainty. Embedded in them is the account of two sins. One, as we have seen, brought a curse on the people as a whole, for the whole camp was involved in the curse the banned articles had brought with them. It is true that in God's grace the penalty was paid by Achan and his family, but something of the effect of the sin continued in the history of the people. The other sin was the pact with the Gibeonites. Here the whole people represented by their leaders were to blame, and this was to be the outstanding sin of the people in the period of the Judges even though the sparing of the Canaanites never seems to have been an official action again.

Most of the remainder of the book contains the title deeds of the tribes. Whether or not the tribal portions were fully conquered, whether or not the authority of Israel stretched to the boundaries set by God, every square inch of the land had been allocated by God. None could take it from them without God's permitting, and where they did not possess all it was a standing testimony to their sin and lack of faith.

JUDGES

Joshua and his younger contemporaries served as a barrier preventing the people from following their own fancies (Jdg. 2: 7), but such barriers all too often serve as dams, and once they are removed or breached there seems no means to check the rush to evil. Lest we should be surprised at the rapidity or apparent completeness of the people's apostasy, Judges begins with a list of the failures of the period of the Conquest, which reveals the true attitude of the people to God – 'After the death of Joshua' indicates the theme of the book, not of ch. 1, for his death is not described until 2: 8, 9.

A superficial reading will make us think that Israel simply turned its back on Jehovah and worshipped the gods of the conquered Canaanites. But this is not the way sane people behave. What they did was much commoner, something to which we too are very prone. The clue is given by Jdg. 2: 10. Of course they knew with their heads what Jehovah had done for Israel, but it did not dominate their lives. He was for them one god among many gods, one power among many powers; He was even the great God, but . . . they did as we so often do. We ascribe to God all power and love, but we feel constrained to compromise and bow down to the gods of this world, wealth, force, human opinion and a good name. The prophetic writers of Judges call it quite simply Baal worship. It should be noted that all our stress on 'correct' worship and church administration will never by themselves create this inner trust in God.

Equally we see that this trust is not really created by punishment and suffering. Though the rule of foreign powers drove the people sooner or later to cry to God in their despair, their deliverance never really created this deep-rooted, all-dominating trust.

As in Joshua this book is not a history of the time, but an account of human sin and God's mighty acts. So once again the attempt to write a history in the modern style on the basis of Judges may well lead to serious misunderstanding. The two appendices, chs. 17, 18 and chs. 19–21, of which the latter is demonstrably earlier than the former (cf. 20: 28), are intended to show us a little of the religious and social declension of the people. But they also indicate to the careful reader that very much is left unsaid in the stories of the deliverers, for to have said it would have been to obscure the main purpose of the stories. It is quite possible that some of the judges had only local influence, and that two or more may have been contemporaries.

For many some of the traits of the heroes of faith mentioned exist only to be explained away. For example they find it impossible to believe that Jephthah could really have offered up his daughter. But one of the great lessons we have to learn about God is that He uses the material at hand. In a rude and crude age it is likely to be rude and crude as was Samson. There are few more offensive and near blasphemous exercises than to allegorize Samson into a type of Christ. It is as bad, and more foolish, to resolve him into a sun myth as do some slightly older commentaries. In his time the average Israelite was oblivious to the growing danger from the

Philistines – cf. the quiet acceptance of their overlordship by
Judah (15: 11). God could not waken the people to their peril,
but He could make and use a man who would use his
superhuman strength in a personal quarrel (15: 3) seriously
to weaken their power. If it is asked how Samson, taken
literally, can be regarded as a hero of faith, the answer is that
however rude and crude he was, yet he clearly recognized
that the source of his strength was in God. There is no
evidence for his ever seeking to take the credit to himself.
Incidentally, it is worth mentioning that Delilah was clearly
an Israelite, else the Philistine lords would not have offered
her such a price (16: 5), and there is no evidence that she was
not Samson's wife.

SAMUEL

The compiler of Samuel has indicated the main divisions
in his book by the use of short summaries from time to time,
viz. 1 Sam. 7: 15–17; 13: 1 (this obviously introductory formula serves the same purpose); 14: 4–52; 2 Sam. 8: 15–18;
20: 23–26. These allow us to speak of the Book of Samuel
(1 Sam. 1–7), the Institution of the Monarchy (1 Sam. 8–12),
the Book of Saul (1 Sam. 13, 14), the Book of David the King
(1 Sam. 15–2 Sam. 8), the Book of David the Man (2 Sam.
9–20) and an Appendix (2 Sam. 21–24).

In the Book of Samuel we see how corrupt religion reached
the heart of Israel in the form it so often takes, viz. sexual
misconduct. With the loss of respect for the priests went the
loss of respect for God. The bringing of the Ark into the camp
of Israel was not a last desperate plea for God's grace, but an
effort to force Him to aid Israel in order to save His throne,
the Ark. The people suffered the worst defeat in their history,
the Ark was taken, the sanctuary at Shiloh was purified by
fire (Jer. 7: 12), but God's honour remained untouched for he
triumphed over the gods of the Philistines by sending the
plague among them, and met the need of Israel by raising up
Samuel, who ranks with Abraham and Moses as one of the
three greatest figures of the Old Testament.

The people could not trust God to raise up a suitable
successor to Samuel, so they demanded a king who would
ensure a firm and certain succession by handing on the

throne to his son. Saul had apparently all that was needed to make an ideal king, but the Bible dismisses his reign contemptuously in two chapters and does not even preserve his age or the length of his reign (cf. 13: 1 in RSV). All that we are told of him from ch. 15 onwards is merely to create the background for the story of David. Chronicles produces the same effect by telling only the story of his death (1 Chr. 10).

With conspicuous skill the writer balances the story of David the successful king with the tragic figure of him as a man, thereby bringing home to us that no man is fit to represent God in the way Israel hoped their king would. The trust, humility and genuine repentance shown by David earn him the commendation of being perfect in heart compared to his successors, but Psa. 51 is David's own judgment on himself.

KINGS

The Book of Kings runs the whole gamut from the meretricious glitter of Solomon's court to the release of the captive king Jehoiachin from his imprisonment in Babylon. We may praise Solomon for choosing wisdom, but very soon we find that his wisdom was merely of the same type as that shown by people in neighbouring lands (1 Ki. 4: 29–31). He had riches in abundance, but he trusted in a marriage alliance with Pharaoh's daughter to protect them, so it was another Pharaoh who removed them all in the next reign (1 Ki. 14: 25, 26). The court lived in luxury, but the people felt the burden of taxation ever more heavily, so his son lost two-thirds of what he had inherited from his father. Solomon was wise, but he forgot the fear of the Lord, and so he went after other gods.

We praise Hezekiah and Josiah for their reformations, but we shall look in vain in Isaiah for a single word of praise for what Hezekiah had done (note also how briefly it is dismissed in Kings), and Jeremiah dismisses Josiah's efforts with a couple of cutting phrases. The heroes of Kings are not the loyal rulers but God's spokesmen, the prophets. What is more, a Jehoshaphat was followed by an Ahaziah, a Hezekiah by a Manasseh, a Josiah by a Jehoiakim. There was no real reformation but a short-lived damming up of evil, which when released only made the final destruction more certain.

SEVEN

The Latter Prophets

IN THE HEBREW BIBLE THE ACCOUNT OF GOD'S DEALINGS WITH HIS apostate people is immediately followed by His words to them through His servants the prophets. These are contained in the four Latter Prophets, viz. Isaiah, Jeremiah, Ezekiel and the Twelve, the latter forming one book in Hebrew. The reason why Daniel does not figure here will be dealt with later in ch. 11.

Just as the Former Prophets do not give a full history of Israel but concern themselves almost exclusively with salvation history, so we do not have a full record of the words of the prophets, but only of those messages that could make later generations wise to salvation. What is more, the arrangement of the prophecies within a book does not necessarily coincide with the chronological order in which they were originally given. When they were first spoken, they were normally brief and in poetry. This was that they might be remembered more easily. The poetic structure is normally indicated in RSV. In addition this translation's indication of paragraph divisions very often, though not always, shows the original brief oracles correctly. Their present arrangement enables us to see far deeper truths in the messages than would have been possible for those who first heard them.

Four things must be grasped if we are to understand and interpret the prophets correctly. First of all they were not philosophers uttering eternal truths in the abstract. They were God's spokesmen in given historical situations. Their messages are still valid today because neither the character of God nor of human sin has changed. Then they were not innovators. Their message was rejected not because it was

novel but because it was unpleasant. They drew out the
deeper implications of the Law even as our Lord did in the
Sermon on the Mount. Thirdly, whenever the message looks
to the future and involves the acceptance or rejection of it by
the hearers, there is an element of contingency in it (Jer.
18: 1–11). This is the reason why numerous predictions about
the future did not go into fulfilment at the time or in the way
that was predicted. (Some of the more striking examples are
Jonah's message to Nineveh; Isa. 16: 13, 14; Ezek. 26: 7–14;
29: 10–12, 17–20.) Finally we must remember that God was
speaking through the prophets in many and various ways
(Heb. 1: 1). That means among other things that God's
fulfilment is always more wonderful than the message itself.

The purpose and size of this book do not allow for a detailed
discussion of the message of each of the prophets.[1] It will,
however, be of value to draw out the outstanding doctrines
they preached.

THE DAY OF THE LORD

Joel is the only prophet whom we cannot date with any
certainty. Although in common with the others he gave his
message against a definite historical background and as a
response to a critical position, it was and remained in essence
timeless. It concerned the Day of the Lord, which is for the
Old Testament what the Second Coming of Christ is for the
New. Nearly all the prophets refer to the Day directly or by
inference, but it is really from Joel that we obtain the
framework which brings them all into intelligible harmony.

The Old Testament prophets are mainly concerned with
that aspect of the Day which we call the Judgment Seat of
Christ. When Peter says that judgment is to begin with the
household of God (1 Pet. 4: 17) he is merely expressing a
dominant note in the Old Testament. If we, relying on the
comparatively few references to it in the New Testament, fail
to give much place to the Judgment Seat, it comes from
inadequate study of the prophetic message.

---

[1] I have done this in my *Men Spoke From God* without much detail,
see also my *The Prophets of Israel* for the Northern Kingdom.

THE LOVE OF GOD

Somewhere in the somewhat less than forty years between the death of Elisha and the preaching of Amos we must place Jonah's visit to Nineveh. Some of those who heard Amos witnessed the destruction of Samaria, so Jonah stands at the beginning of the period that heads up to inevitable judgment.

That God should chastise His people and that through the scourge of the foreigner was something that created no problem for the thinking Israelite. But that He should give up His people to the death of exile was something almost incredible. We find Hosea wrestling with the problem:

> How can l give you up, O Ephraim!
> How can I hand you over, O Israel!'
> (Hos. 11: 8).

It was necessary that Israel, and then Judah in its turn should learn that the God who judges and punishes is also the God who loves.

In this remarkable book we find Him not merely seeking the repentance of the evil city of Nineveh but also yearning over the 'hundred and twenty thousand persons who do not know their right hand from their left' (presumably the children) 'and also much cattle.'

We are still in need of this message. We are still so under the spell of 'standard Calvinism' that while we do not doubt God's beneficent rule over the world and affirm the truth of Rom. 8: 28 without hesitation, we also assume that God is well pleased to allow the majority of men to go to eternal death. There cannot be salvation outside Christ, otherwise He would not have died. There must be freedom for a man to choose eternal death, else he would not be truly man. But we must be prepared to believe also that God's love and wisdom are 'broader than the measures of man's mind'. This is the preparation Jonah gives us for the oracles of judgment that follow.

THE EIGHTH-CENTURY PROPHETS

It is usual to bring together the prophecies of Amos, Hosea, Isaiah 1–39 and Micah under the general title of the

Eighth-Century prophets. If Isa. 40–66 is not dealt with under this title, it is not because I doubt the Isaianic authorship, but because the outstanding message of these chapters is best taken in another setting.

The dominating message of these prophets, irrespective of whether they are addressing the North or Judah, is the justification of the coming judgment. The outstanding reason given is the injustice and inhumanity of the great and powerful towards the weak, poor and helpless. The first and great commandment is 'You shall love the Lord your God with all your heart, and with all your soul, and with all your might.' For all that it remains true, 'if any one says, "I love God," and hates his brother, he is a liar; for he who does not love his brother whom he has seen, cannot love God whom he has not seen' (1 John 4: 20). It is not given to us to anticipate the great day of judgment and the charges that will be brought against men then, but the sins that the prophets charged Israel with were open and undeniable, and from them the people's attitude towards God could be inferred.

For Amos the fundamental characteristic of God was justice. This justice would be displayed against those that sinned against their own conscience, even though they were not members of the covenant people. How much more then could Israel expect to experience the justice of God when it sinned against the light. He was little concerned with Israel's religious practices, for whether they were correct or not, they could not replace the fundamental demand of justice in life.

Hosea was more concerned with his people's doings in the light of God's love. He had through his own broken family life learnt the sufferings of love when faced with infidelity. He looked on the sins of the mighty as they ground the poor in the dust as above all a violation of love, for they were all members of God's family elected in love. The faults in Israel's religion he looked on less as a violation of regulations laid down than as a debasing of the image and concept of the God who had freed them from slavery in Egypt and made them His people. He saw, as Amos apparently never did, the cost to God in condemning His people, but he also saw that it was a contradiction in terms that a people without love to God should be God's people in full possession of all their privileges.

For most of us it is very hard to bring justice and love together. We so often give the impression that we are denying or depreciating one or the other. Isaiah was able to bring the two together in his vision of the holiness of God. On the one hand His love goes out to all He has made, so that 'the whole earth is full of His glory'. On the other His justice separates Him from sinful man. The answer to this apparent contradiction he saw in the Remnant. He realized that physical descent in itself was insufficient to create the people of God. That title could rightly be borne only by the 'holy seed' within it, which, as had Isaiah himself, had experienced guilt removed and sin forgiven (Isa. 6: 7). The revelation of how this could happen came to him much later in life, and this will be considered later.

Isaiah foresaw the cutting down both of the national tree (Isa. 6: 13, RV or RSV!) and of the royal tree (Isa. 11: 1). With the remnant people would appear the king who would be all that David and his successors had never been (Isa. 9: 2–7; 11: 1–9). But this is precisely the difference between Isaiah and Elijah. For the latter the failure of the people was evidence that God's plans had failed (1 Ki. 19: 14). The former, however, was able to see that the perfect fulfilment of God's purposes was linked with and sprang out of the apparent failure of contemporary Israel.

Micah is the one of these four prophets who at first makes least impact on the average reader. It is striking, however, that he is the only one of them of whom it is recorded that his message brought about any reformation, however transient (Jer. 26: 17–19). This was probably because he was an insignificant citizen (his father's name is not mentioned) of an insignificant provincial market town. He himself had evidently experienced the oppression of the rich in his own person and so spoke of it with a crude power that even the polish of the AV cannot really weaken and so shocked King Hezekiah into action. Quite understandably and fittingly his prophecies of the coming Messianic king stress his humble origins.

To him was given to proclaim the moral demands of God in language that remains unequalled:

> 'He has showed you, O man, what is good;
>   and what does the Lord require of you
> but to do justice, and to love loyal love,
>   and to walk humbly with your God.'

'To do justice' is, of course a summing up of Amos' message, and equally 'to love loyal love' represents Hosea. 'To walk humbly with your God' expresses the result of a true understanding of the holiness of God as Isaiah experienced and preached it.

THE DAYS OF JOSIAH

There is a gap of well over half a century between Isaiah and Micah and the three prophets Nahum, Zephaniah and Habakkuk, with whom Jeremiah could be linked; it will he more profitable, however, to consider him along with Ezekiel and the later prophecies of Isaiah.

There is no evidence that God raised up any prophets in the fifty-five years of Manasseh's reign. The tradition that he had Isaiah murdered may well be true. But the eighth-century prophets had done their work well. No doubt about God's will remained. If Manasseh would not listen to their message he would not listen to a new prophet, and so apparently none were sent to him.

Zephaniah, who may even have been of royal blood, though this is unprovable – his long genealogy (Zeph. 1: 1) shows that he came of a family of importance – was the harbinger of a new age. The evil heaped upon evil during Manasseh's reign called for a reaffirmation of the judgment of the Day of the Lord and also of the blessing to follow. Since the description in Zeph. 1 clearly dates from before the beginnings of Josiah's reformation, we may with confidence see in the prophet the one who moved the young king to begin his reformation.

Nahum occupies a complementary position to Jonah. The latter showed God's love in its longsuffering seeking the repentance and salvation of wicked Nineveh. Nahum reveals the consequences of flouting that love. Nineveh, once spared in the mercy of God, now goes down to even more complete ruin.

Habakkuk occupies a unique place in the roll of God's prophets. It is not even clear how far the contents of his book were preached to the men of his time. We have the impression that we have the record of a dialogue between the prophet and God stretching over a number of years. He recognized that the conditions of the time called for severest judgment

(Hab. 1: 2–4); describing conditions under 'good' king Josiah! Yet, as is so often the case today, he could not reconcile God's judgment with the instruments used for inflicting it. It is to be noted that the question of Hab. 1: 13 is not answered either here or elsewhere in Scripture. There are mysteries in the Divine rule into which not even prophets are allowed to penetrate.

Habakkuk's great contribution to the growing volume of revealed truth is 'The righteous shall live by his faithfulness' (Hab. 2: 4). This translation is necessary, if we are to be true to the Hebrew. The Israelite in his concrete outlook on life did not speak of faith; no man can really show his faith except through his faithfulness to God. Otherwise faith remains a pale abstraction of uncertain meaning. The traditional translation is to accommodate it to the Greek of Romans. It is to be noted that Habakkuk speaks of the individual. He could already see the axe lifted up to hew down both the national and the royal trees, but he received the revelation that in the uncertainties of the remnant the individual remained safe through a life living out his inner trust in God.

JEREMIAH

Among the prophets whose message has been recorded for us Jeremiah stands unique for the extent to which his life forms part of his book. Indeed, he is the only prophet for whom one could write a partial biography. The fact is that in him life and message coalesce in a measure that is approached only in a slight degree in Hosea.

It is impossible for man really to foresee the completely unexpected and never previously experienced. Many an individual Israelite and family had disappeared into slavery in some foreign land before the leading families of the northern tribes looked their last on their homeland as they were led away by the Assyrian soldiery. It is clear the common people were left behind. But through all this the services of the Jerusalem sanctuary had gone on uninterruptedly. Even when the Rabshakeh mouthed his threats outside the walls of Jerusalem in the reign of Hezekiah, even when the idols and altars erected by Manasseh almost hid the true furniture of the Temple, the Jerusalem priesthood continued its functions.

It seemed as though there were one sure, unshaken central point amid all the troubles of life. It is not in the least surprising that the people, led by the priests and prophets, wanted to lynch Jeremiah, when he foretold the destruction of the Temple (26: 1–19; 7: 1–15).

We can see from *Lamentations* something of the shock the destruction of Jerusalem and its temple brought with it. The air of despair and hopelessness that breathes through most of this short book is a fair means to measure it by. It was necessary, therefore, that God should raise up a demonstration that through grace a man could live a life of trust when every outward help and stay had been removed; this He did through Jeremiah.

With the imminence of judgment the shadows in Jeremiah's oracles may be deeper than in many of those of his predecessors, but in the prophecies as a whole there is little that is new. At the same time the superficiality of Josiah's reformation has led to probably the deepest conception of repentance in the Old Testament. This has been obscured in the English translations of 4: 3, which should be rendered, 'Break up your virgin soil'. No amount of turning to the past ('fallow ground') or turning over a new leaf would suffice. It had to be a completely new beginning.

During the first five years of Jehoiakim's reign we see Jeremiah suffering blow after blow. First the people rejected his message and sought his life (26: 1–19). Then the men of his home village, Anathoth, instigated by his own family, tried to murder him (11: 18–12: 6). We find him bitterly reviled and maligned (15: 10–18), unmarried and alone (16: 1–4), his position aggravated by God's prohibition against his joining in the sorrows and joys of his neighbours (16: 5–9). Perhaps his biggest shock was to find the religious leaders listening to his message merely to find a handle for attacking him (18: 18–23). Then he had the experience of being flogged and put in the stocks (20: 2) and being refused entrance to the Temple (36: 5, RSV). To crown it all he had to go underground to escape Jehoiakim's fury (36: 26). Jeremiah almost collapsed but not quite (20: 7–18). As the clouds of retribution gathered round Jehoiakim, Jeremiah was back at his post (ch. 35), which he did not forsake in the face of starvation, imprisonment and slow death in the dry cistern (38: 1–13). Where others would have sought a few years in retirement, he clung to his people and went with them to Egypt, where he presumably died.

It is against this background that we must interpret the promise of the new covenant (31: 31–34). So far as it was possible for anyone to do it before Christ, Jeremiah experienced its blessing and power, while he demonstrated that it was possible for a man to walk in God's ways, even when he had been stripped of every human stay. The people could believe the promise because he made it real, and he must have made exile very much more bearable for many.

EZEKIEL

Jeremiah prophesied to those who were to go into exile, Ezekiel to those who were already there. His task was largely to convince them that their presence in exile was an act of astounding grace on God's part. It was not God's punishment on them as the blackest of the black, but the only way in which He could save them from the inevitable doom that was coming on Jerusalem. This involved his giving of the past history of Israel in the darkest colours used anywhere in the Old Testament. In fact there are very few even today who are prepared to give full weight to chs. 16, 20, 23, though they are vital to the understanding of the Old Testament as a whole. The view that the Bible shows us man's growing discovery and apprehension of God is based on humanist evolutionary ideas of how things ought to have been and not on the Bible, but even among those who realize this there will be many who think that the Old Testament gives us a picture of progress. In fact the destruction of Jerusalem by Nebuchadnezzar is God's verdict on its earlier portion and that by Titus on its later part.

Just because of this, his appreciation of the new covenant goes in some ways very much deeper than Jeremiah's (36: 24–27). For the same reason he rearranged and reconstructed the whole scheme of restoration which runs through the earlier prophets. There it is always apostasy, judgment, repentance, restoration. Through Jeremiah the virtual human impossibility of repentance had been made clear, and so in Ezekiel the scheme becomes changed to apostasy, judgment, restoration and repentance, and the last is based on God's gracious activity alone.

This scheme is folly to those who are guided by human concepts of what is fitting, as may be seen by so many Christian comments on the State of Israel. It is suggested that it cannot be of God because there has not been the necessary preliminary repentance by the Jews. The simple fact is that certain aspects of God's working are so contrary to human wisdom, that they cannot be revealed until the inadequacy of man has first been laid bare.

For this reason, more than with most of the prophets, the return in Ezekiel clearly falls into the last days, the days of the Messiah. There is no evidence that those who returned in the reign of Cyrus considered that they were fulfilling the prophecies of Ezekiel.

It is in itself perhaps of small importance how we interpret Ezek. 40–48. Some see in it a blue print of the Temple and its worship, when Christ reigns visibly over men after His return. Many more find that this raises so many intolerable spiritual and exegetical difficulties that they interpret the chapters symbolically, finding in them a revelation of the truth which reaches its climax in the New Jerusalem of Rev. 21, 22. In either case the transformation of man under the new covenant implies the introduction of God's perfect plan and order. The fact that those who returned from exile apparently ignored these chapters is the best evidence that they did not think they applied to them.

THE SERVANT OF THE LORD

Though the arguments for denying the Isaianic authorship of Isa. 40–45 are probably far weaker that those who use them normally realize, there is a real advantage in considering the message of these chapters here. (Chs. 56-66 link either with chs. 1–3 or 40–55 according to their contents, and so they need no special consideration here.) Whatever the reason why chs. 40–55 may not have been given through a prophet of the exile, they presuppose the exile. They are spoken not to those who are to go into exile, or even to their ancestors, but to those who actually find themselves there.

In chs. 40–48 we have a picture of Jehovah, the All-

Sovereign, who is about to bring a new Exodus into being. We see Him as the controller alike of nature and of kings in the accomplishment of His purposes. This section ends with Israel freed from the dominion of Babylon, but not from that of sin. Chs. 49–55 are concerned with how Israel, the blind and deaf servant of the Lord, can be freed from sin. So we are introduced to the true Servant, who is all that Israel should have been and never was, who does all that Israel longed to do and never could. He is the Remnant to whom the remnant had pointed.

History shows us that there were only a few in Israel who had begun to take this revelation seriously by the time of our Lord, and there is no evidence that any of these had penetrated into its real meaning. There are elements in it that baffled men before Jesus of Nazareth made it luminous by fulfilling it. Even so today it baffles those that refuse to see Him as its fulfiller. In these Servant passages we find traits of the king, of the prophet and of the high priest so united that they point to the only one who was truly all three.

THE POST-EXILIC PROPHETS

After the return from exile the office of prophet rapidly faded out. For this there were various reasons. On the popular side the prophets who had been denounced by men like Jeremiah and Ezekiel had been hopelessly discredited by the destruction of Jerusalem. The tragic end to their optimistic foretellings had ended in complete disaster, and so they were shown up as men who had never stood in God's council chamber (Jer. 23: 18, 21, 22). On a somewhat higher level the prophet was no longer felt to be essential, once the people had come to know the Law through Ezra's reform (Neh. 8: 1–18). On the highest level, however, the prophet had to disappear because there was no more for God to reveal until the Fulfiller of prophecy should come. The three whose words have been preserved for us, Haggai, Zechariah and Malachi, form the bridge between the prophetic revelation and the sermon.

It is only in the last section of Haggai (2: 20–23) that we have the normal prophetic formula, 'the word of the Lord came to Haggai'; elsewhere (1: 1, 3; 2: 1, 10) the unusual formula 'the word of the Lord came by Haggai' (cf. also 1: 12,

13) is found. In a sphere where expressions had become stereotyped the change implied a change in the type of message. It is clear that Haggai was applying Spirit-given logic based on the revelation given in the past to the situation then existing. His message to Zerubbabel, on the other hand, was not deducible from the past, and so it fell into the sphere of normal prophecy.

In the first six chapters of Zechariah we meet a type of prophecy which is technically known as apocalyptic and is particularly associated with Daniel and Revelation (cf. ch. 11). It was only comparatively little used by his prophetic predecessors. It is less concerned with the spiritual position of its first hearers and more with the working out of God's purposes in the future. In other words the post-exilic community was being called to live out its life in trust in the revealed future purposes of God. It had all the revelation of the character of God it needed or could grasp until the perfect Revealer should come. Much the same can be said of the main contents of the concluding chapters of the book, which may well be the work of an anonymous prophet of the same period.

Much of the great popularity of Malachi in certain circles in the pulpit and on the platform is explicable by his messages being the nearest approach to a series of short sermons in the Old Testament. The modern expositor normally finds that he need do no more than explain an expression here and there, emphasize the prophet's points and apply them to the changed circumstances of today.

Both in the past and today there have been few who doubted that Malachi, which means 'My messenger', should either be so translated in 1: 1, or should be regarded as a title assumed by the prophet. In either case it is not a proper name. This in itself is a sign of the transition from the clearly marked individuality of the prophet to the far greater anonymity of the preacher.

EIGHT

The Psalter

QUITE RIGHTLY AND SPIRITUALLY LOGICALLY THE HEBREW BIBLE places the Psalter at the beginning of the Writings (cf. Luke 24: 44) and so immediately after the Prophets. After God has spoken to men through the prophets they should in turn speak to Him as they are moved by the Spirit.

The failure to realize that the Psalter is essentially a record of Israel's speaking to God has led to strange efforts to interpret it prophetically. Though there is an element, and an important element, of truth in this view, as we shall see later, only two of the psalms, viz. 50 and 110, lay claim by their form to be regarded as prophecy in the full sense.

With few exceptions (e.g. Psa. 119), the psalms were composed to be sung, and that in the worship of the Temple. To what extent they were linked with the Temple is seen in the fact that the Synagogue, in spite of the range and richness of its worship, has found use for only about two of them. On the other hand there is little difficulty in fitting most of them into the ritual of the burnt offering, of the peace offering, of the sin and guilt offerings, of the great fast days, and into the great royal ceremonies. One smaller collection (120–134) has taken psalms from their original setting and has applied them to the use of pilgrims coming up to Jerusalem for the great festivals.

THE OVERRULING OF INDIVIDUAL PERSONALITY

Many, especially among the psalms of David, quite obviously sprang from situations of intense personal suffering and need, but the manner in which that suffering and need have found their expression has been overruled by the Holy Spirit. A hymn that does not spring from personal experience will never be a good one, but one that expresses only personal experience will be an even worse hymn, however great religious poetry it may be. For the hymn to be really great the personal experience behind it must be so generalized that it can be used honestly and feelingly by a wide section of the average worshipping community. A good example is Charles Wesley's 'And can it be that 1 should gain?'; few who sing it realize that it was the immediate product of his conversion experience.

It is often claimed that David could never have written many of the psalms that bear his name, because it seems impossible to fit them into the framework of the known facts about his life. The same difficulty is often felt even when the title reveals the setting. There seems to be little relationship between the two.

Quite so! Just therein lies their greatness. If they were constantly reminding us of David's troubles and joys, we should find it much more difficult to use them as a vehicle to express our own. That this difficulty was felt even then is shown by the adaptation of some of the most individualistic of them for public worship, e.g. in Psa. 51 this was done by the addition of verses 18, 19.

TWO MAIN TYPES OF PSALMS

The lack of a title to Psa. 2, although the Davidic authorship was commonly accepted (Acts 4: 25), is most easily explained by its being, in its present position, along with Psa. 1, which may even have been written for the purpose, an introduction to the Psalter as a whole. The two cover all but a very few of the contents.

On the one hand, represented by Psa. 1, we have the psalms of God's man. We see him in all his sorrows and joys, defeats and victories, fears and triumphs. Sometimes we have these psalms in the singular, which may, according to circumstances, represent the voice of an individual or of the community as personified in an individual. This is one of the reasons why we sometimes have an alternation between singular and plural. On the other hand we may find the community speaking in the plural.

Psa. 2, on the other hand, represents the psalms of God's king. It is not always easy to draw the dividing line between them. This is partly because the king was looked on as representative of the community. Then, in many of the Davidic psalms it is often difficult to decide whether he is speaking as an individual before his God, or whether he approaches the throne of God as the one who sits on God's throne on earth.

Since the man of God in the Old Testament repeatedly *foreshadows* in some measure God's perfect Man, both through his trials and his communion with God, just as we in turn reflect His perfect life, most of the psalms in the first group foreshadow in some measure the Coming One. But there is a great difference between foreshadowing and prophecy.

A couple of examples must suffice. We see no contradiction, for there is none, in applying Psa. 40: 1–3 to our own experience, but verses 6–8 to our Lord's. Surely, however, these latter verses apply in some measure both to David and to us who are written in the Lamb's Book of Life (Rev. 13: 8). Equally we can reverently apply verses 1–3 to our Lord, though with a far deeper meaning than when they are our own personal testimony. What we cannot do by any form of reverent exegesis is to apply,

> My iniquities have overtaken me,
>   till 1 cannot see;
> they are more than the hairs of my head;
>   my heart fails me (v. 12),

to Jesus Christ, though there are those who attempt it to the great spiritual discomfort of most who hear them. Even in Psa. 22, though David had been led through his own suffering and deliverance and had been taught to express them in terms of a greater suffering and deliverance, yet there remain phrases that are peculiarly David's, which the sensitive heart will shrink from applying to Christ.

Things are somewhat different when we turn to the royal psalms. Partly because of contemporary Near-Eastern concepts, but far more because of the promise to David recorded in 2 Sam. 7: 16, Israel was very conscious of the part the king should play, but at the best fulfilled only partially. Yet he was always the promise of the yet future king who would be all that the kings should have been. Hence repeatedly in these psalms language was used which all concerned knew would and indeed could not be fulfilled in the one being celebrated. Whether at his coronation or at its anniversary celebrations the king was thus reminded of the ideals towards which he should strive, ideals which a member of the house of David would one day fulfil. There is no reason for doubting that Psa. 110 was used at coronations, but the self-evident fact that the king was not 'a priest for ever after the order of Melchizedek' was sufficient to show that it was an oracle concerning a king yet to come.[1] All this makes the royal psalms much easier to apply to our Lord, but even then there remain obstinate elements in them which refuse to fit the picture of Christ, even after the most artistic allegorization. This in itself should show us that, except in Psa. 110, we are not dealing with direct prophecy.

ASCRIPTIONS OF AUTHORSHIP

Though in our devotional use of the Psalter the authorship of a psalm will seldom prove to be of much importance, yet the title or lack of title with a psalm may well help us in finding its deeper meanings. Even the division into books can guide us. In Hebrew, although this is not indicated in normal editions of the Authorized Version, the Psalter is divided into five books, viz. Pss. 1–41; 42–72; 73–89; 90–106; 107–150. This was doubtless to correspond with the five books of Moses, though no parallelism in the contents should be looked for. Today, however, it is generally believed that originally there were only three, viz. Pss. 1–41; 42–89; 90–150. If we accept this, we can label the three collections, although only approximately correctly, Davidic, Levitical and Anonymous. There are, of course, Davidic and anonymous psalms in all three collections.

---

[1] The confident statement in some modern text-books that David did indeed become such a priest when he captured Jerusalem and took over its priesthood cannot appeal to the least trace of evidence.

The number of the Psalms, 150, is quite accidental. The Greek translation has an extra one, the Hebrew original of which has been found among the fragments in the Qumran library – there is nothing in its quality that will lead to any agitation for its inclusion in our versions. In addition Pss. 9 and 10 are one psalm, as is shown by the acrostic running through them; 42 and 43 are also obviously one. In addition Psa. 53, apart from the change of Jehovah to God, is a virtual doublet of Psa. 14, and Psa. 70 is merely verses 13–17 of Psa. 40, again with some changes in the Divine name. Psa. 108 is a linking of Psa. 57: 7–11 and Psa. 60: 5–12.

Whether or not the author's name is given depends normally on the contents of the individual psalm. Where a knowledge of authorship can help us in any way to understand the contents better, the name is usually given; where nothing is to be gained from it, it is normally omitted. Hence the anonymous psalms are mostly hymns of worship; where they praise God for His goodness, it is normally for time past, not for the author's own time. A comparison of Pss. 100 and 103 should make this clear. In the former there is nothing that could not be said by any true believer at any time. In the latter, verses 3–5 mirror David's own personal experience, as is made even clearer by the Hebrew original.

It would also appear to be quite accidental in which collection certain psalms appear. There is little doubt that Pss. 6, 38, 51, 32, in this order, are linked with the period after David's sin with Bathsheba, yet their chronological order and connection are ignored, and Psa. 51 appears in the second collection, while the other three are in the first. This is a warning against reading a deeper meaning into the actual order of the psalms. Where this is indulged in, the speaker should acknowledge that he is drawing on his fancy, not on the Spirit's guidance of the compiler of the Psalter. Normally a psalm is as complete in itself as is a modern hymn.

If we include Psa. 2 there are 74 psalms attributed to David, but in the Greek translation there are several more. There are no grounds whatever for attributing these extra headings to the translators themselves; they will have found them in the manuscripts they used. Since we set very little store by these extra attributions, it seems clear that already then there was the tendency to claim David as the author of anonymous psalms. So we are justified in thinking that some of the psalms attributed to David may not be by him. Psa. 86 may not be, though since the writer used so much Davidic material we may as well let the attribution stand. It seems difficult to attribute Psa. 69 to him. There is so much in it that we can hardly fit into his life; in addition the whole tone of the psalm is different. It would be far easier to think of Jeremiah as its author. Though in itself there are no objections to a Davidic authorship of Psa. 65, it becomes historically much more intelligible if we can place it in the time of Hezekiah.

Apart from the serene thanksgiving of Psa. 103 and Psa. 65 (if indeed it is by David), the dark thread of his enemies, who are also God's enemies, runs throughout the Davidic psalms. Wicked men are found in other psalms, including Psa. 69, but their writers' attitude towards them is different. There they are an evil to be endured and from whom one is to be delivered. With David they are an affront and a challenge to his standing as God's anointed. One might say that where a Christian might speak of Satan, David is concerned with those who act as Satan's agents. He realizes that they are more than evil, for they serve the powers of evil.

It is obvious enough that the Psalms of the Sons of Korah have a number of authors. Psa. 44, with its protestations of innocence, can best be dated in the time of David, while Psa. 45 seems to mirror that of Solomon. Pss. 42 and 43 (one psalm) must come from the time of Jeroboam 1, and be written by a Levite who found himself stranded near Dan, cut off from the Jerusalem temple. It is quite possible that he may have written Psa. 84 after he had moved to Judah. The majority, however, come from the time of Hezekiah and celebrate the deliverance of the city and Temple from Senacherib. Psa. 49, though it may have been sung to pilgrims at the great festivals, was quite obviously not composed for use at the sacrificial services.

In the same way the psalms of Asaph come from a family of Levitical singers. Pss. 75, 76, 80 can be dated with reasonable certainty in the reign of Hezekiah, like the similar Korahite psalms. Pss. 79, 74, in that order, must surely be dated after the destruction of Jerusalem by Nebuchadnezzar. There is no indication of the date of the remaining Asaphite psalms. Pss. 77, 73, in that order, come from the same man. We shall probably not be far wrong, if we place Psa. 50 in the time of Hezekiah, for there are considerable similarities of thought with Isaiah. It is in the Psalter only because there was no prophetic book of Asaph. In the same way the musical directions in Hab. 3 suggest that it was once in one of the collections of psalms, but that it was transferred to its present position just because its author had his prophetic book. It is interesting that the Qumran people quite clearly did not regard it as part of Habakkuk's *prophecy*.

There are good grounds for thinking that Pss. 93–100 are a small collection of psalms used chiefly at the feast of Tabernacles, when the sovereignty of God was especially celebrated both as it was seen in nature and also in the continuance of the Davidic dynasty. Naturally the latter thought fell out after the Babylonian exile. Equally Pss. 113–118 (the *Hallel*) are a collection for the Passover, which later in the Synagogue was used also for the other great festivals.

We may consider a few modern hymns almost worthy to be placed on the same level as the Psalter, for surely the Holy Spirit has been active in many of our hymn writers. It is undeniable, however, that when we regard the Psalter as a whole, no later hymn book can stand any real comparison with it. That is why the Church has always felt that the Psalter has a basic place in its worship, though in practice this truth is all too often forgotten.

NINE

The Wisdom Books

A FEATURE OF THE OLD TESTAMENT IS THAT IT HAS SOMETHING TO tell us of all man's main concerns in life. Hence, although its major portion is given up to God's revelation of Himself to man, it also contains books which throw light on man's varying reactions to the situations in which he finds himself.

When man is compared with animals, his outstanding characteristic is that he is a rational being, able to understand events, to compare similar happenings in the present and past and to draw valid conclusions from them for the future. This is the basis of all man's scientific knowledge, but the Bible is not concerned with this aspect of his rationality. It confines itself to man's efforts to understand God's moral government of the world.

Abraham's question, 'Shall not the Judge of all the earth do right?' (Gen. 18: 25) shows that at even that early date the existence of a moral purpose to the world was recognized and that men considered that they could grasp it, at least in measure. Obviously Abraham was implying that he could recognize what was right.

Man's thoughts on these subjects are found in three of the Old Testament books, viz. Proverbs, Job and Ecclesiastes, or Qohelet, as it is called in Hebrew. Scholars are accustomed to bring them together under the heading Wisdom Literature. In the Apocrypha there are two similar books, The Wisdom of Jesus ben Sira, the Hebrew original of which dates from about 180 B.C., and The Wisdom of Solomon (written about 100 B.C.). These two will not be further mentioned here.

PROVERBS

The wisdom which man gained by his study of the past and present was in Israel, and in the Ancient Near East generally, normally expressed in short, pithy sentences, which might be reinforced by a parallel statement, or more commonly pointed by one showing the reverse. An example of the former is,

> 'He who corrects a scoffer gets himself abuse,
> and he who reproves a wicked man incurs injury'
> (Prov. 9: 7)

and of the latter

> A wise son makes a glad father,
> but a foolish son is a sorrow to his mother'
> (Prov. 10: 1).

The vast majority of the book of Proverbs consists of such parallel statements. In addition it is really a collection of collections of proverbs.

If 1: 1–7 is, as is almost certainly the case, a general introduction to the book. then the first of the collections is 1 : 8–9: 18. It is then anonymous and probably the latest written. The strongest indication of this is its very much more elaborate structure compared with the two indubitably Solomonic collections.

The first Solomonic collection (10: 1–22: 16) contains 375 proverbs, corresponding to the numerical value of the letters of the king's name. This suggests that it was a deliberate effort to collect the best of his maxims. The second Solomonic collection (25: 1–29: 27) was made without any close reference to the first, for a number of proverbs from the older collection are repeated in it.

In 22: 17–24: 22 we have a collection of proverbs from the Wise. As the Septuagint shows, 'my words' has dropped from the original text of 22: 17, which was:

> 'The Words of the Wise.
> Incline your ears and hear my words,
> and apply your mind to my knowledge.'

It is quite typical that this section has a good deal to say about proper behaviour in the presence of kings and rulers. To this has been added a shorter collection headed 'These also are sayings of the Wise' (24: 23–34).

The book of Proverbs is terminated by three short sections, The Words of Agur (30: 1–33), The Words of Lemuel (31: 1–9), and an acrostic poem on the ideal wife (31: 10–31).

With the exception of the short section attributed to Agur, the outlook of Proverbs is homogeneous. Throughout it is assumed that God's moral order can easily be understood by those that are wise. No claim is made that this wisdom is a natural endowment. It is a knowledge derived from the fear of the Lord combined with a moral walk (compare 1: 7; 2: 5 with 8: 13 and 9: 10). Folly and ignorance, as used in Proverbs, are not due to mental retardation or lack of education; they are the morally culpable results of refusing to acquire wisdom.

The moral order pictured is marked out by the prosperity and long life of the good, moral, law-abiding and wise, and by the suffering, poverty and early death of the wicked. The natural inference is that we can judge a man's character by the type of reward or punishment he receives in this life.

Agur stands out against this superficial and optimistic view. He first depreciates his own abilities and knowledge in the true tradition of Oriental courtesy (30: 2, 3), and then affirms that God's ways and nature are essentially unknowable. He reinforces his viewpoint by appealing to the incomprehensibility of so much that we meet in normal life.

There is a certain amount of Wisdom poetry in the Psalter, the most important example being Psa. 49. Since, however, the attitude taken up is essentially the same as in Proverbs, there is no need to make further mention of it.

THE BOOK OF JOB

At first glance no book might seem further from the rather prosaic morality and admonitions of Proverbs than the flaming protests and poetry of Job. In fact, in their inner purpose they stand very close together however diverse their form. The unknown author of Job took an age-old story and reclothed it in some of the finest poetry of the Bible, indeed of the literature of mankind. The essential point to grasp is that while Job before his disasters and his three friends were very wealthy chiefs and rulers, yet it is primarily as members of the Wise that they are depicted, and their words, even at their most passionate, echo the discussions of the Wise throughout the Near East.

The three friends show marked differences. For Eliphaz the Temanite the most important thing is God-given experience rightly understood; Bildad the Shuhite is a venerator of the traditional wisdom of the past; Zophar the Naamathite displays common sense at its most brutal. Yet all their arguments are ultimately those that could at any time have been heard among the Wise. Equally in Job's words we can ever and again recognize the teaching he had been reared in. His real suffering came not from his losses and his illness, but because his experience did not tally with the theories he had learnt. It seemed to him that the moral foundations of the world had collapsed, and that his rudderless boat was being driven on an uncharted sea. In Elihu we hear the inherited wisdom of the aristocratic young man who had had no formal training in these matters.[1]

God's answer to Job – He does not trouble about the theories of his friends – seems at first sight to be no answer at all, and it certainly throws no new light on His moral principles and purposes. He simply challenges him to match His power and understand His wisdom in creation. Yet this obviously satisfies the sufferer, for it brings him to realize that it was not the moral order that had broken down. It was he who had been too puny and shortsighted to grasp it in all its width and wisdom. If in the final chapter Job is restored and more than restored, it is not intended as a vindication of the popular view. God knew that nothing less would conquer the invincible ignorance and prejudice both of Job's friends and of his fellow-townsmen.

It is very important to realize that Job is in the canon of Scripture primarily that its teaching may supplement that of Proverbs. Since the study of Delitzsch on the book there can have been very few who any longer placed its writing before the time of Solomon. Whether we date it then or at any other

[1] I have worked out these points in detail in *From Tragedy to Triumph*.

time down to the third century BC depends mainly on personal bias. Most experience agrees with the picture given by Proverbs, with Job's friends rather than with Job himself. Yet ever and again something happens to show us that there are things in life which cannot be explained by the wisdom of Proverbs. It is then that Job turns us to a God who acts according to principle, but a principle too great and exalted for His actions and motives to be fully grasped and understood.

ECCLESIASTES (*QOHELET*)

Qohelet is for many supremely the mystery book of the Old Testament. Today there are very few who have studied the book who are prepared to defend the apparent Solomonic authorship. Delitzsch's dictum is incontrovertible, 'If Qohelet was written by Solomon, then the Hebrew language has no history'. Its language is an early form of the Hebrew we find in the rabbinic writings of AD 200 and altogether different in style from that of Proverbs and the historical writings from the time of the united monarchy. In addition, cryptic remarks like 1: 1 (why is the name of Solomon not mentioned?), 1: 12 (Solomon never abdicated, as the text suggests!), 1: 16; 2: 9 (David was his only predecessor), 12: 9, 10 (an unlikely description of Solomon) suggest that the author never intended the apparent claims to Solomonic authorship to be taken seriously.

The simplest explanation is that the author, living probably between 250 and 200 BC, placed himself in the shoes of the old, apostate king, who, in spite of his wisdom had gone after other gods – 'the wisest fool in Israel', as he has been called. He is not an atheist, but in spite of his wisdom, he cannot normally understand God's working; the fear of the Lord is lacking. Taken in this way Qohelet is of the utmost importance, for it is the emphatic repudiation of all human wisdom, however great, where the fear of the Lord is lacking. It explains also the occasional passage, especially 12: 13, 14, where there might seem to be a contradiction of the general trend of the book. In fact, the author is here giving the fundamental lesson he has learned from his quest: 'Fear God and keep His commandments'.

So the three wisdom books of the Old Testament belong together and must be interpreted by one another. They are all needed, if we are to obtain God's verdict on human reason and wisdom. They teach us that man may discover much, but not all about God, but that his research will be valid only if it is carried out in the fear of the Lord.

TEN

The Five Scrolls

IN THE HEBREW BIBLE THE *Ketubim* (WRITINGS) CONTAIN A GROUP of five small books known as the *Megillot*, or Scrolls. Apart from the Psalms they are the only portion of the *Ketubim* to be read in the Synagogue, and they are arranged according to their use in the religious year, viz. The Song of Songs, or Canticles, read at Passover, Ruth at Pentecost, Lamentations at the fast of *Tisha b'Ab*, Ecclesiastes on the Day of Atonement, and Esther at Purim.

Ecclesiastes, which deals with the vanity of human wisdom and striving, was considered in ch. 9 in connection with the Wisdom books, so it will not be dealt with further here. Its appositeness for the Day of Atonement is obvious enough.

THE SONG OF SONGS

The opening verse does not necessarily imply authorship by Solomon. It goes no further than to affirm a definite but unspecified link between the poem and Solomon the king. Hence in our interpretation of it we do not have to start from any particular theory of authorship.

Its oldest *official* interpretation was allegorical. It seems certain that when questions were raised about its canonicity at the rabbinic council at Jamnia (*c*.A.D. 90), it was because portions were being used in a literal sense as songs at banquets and possible even in taverns. A little later a curse was pronounced on those that so used it. The rabbis saw in it an allegorical picture of God's love to Israel, though there was no fixed interpretation of the various portions.

The book is not quoted in the New Testament, but from the first its use by the Church Fathers was allegorical. There is only one name of importance in the early period with a literal interpretation, viz. Theodore of Mopsuestia (c.350–428). This probably played some part in his ecclesiastical condemnation after his death. In the Christian view the bride was either the Church or the Virgin Mary. From the Reformation on we increasingly meet the interpretation that in the bride we should see the individual believer rather than the collective Church.

These has never been any consensus of opinion as to how the allegorically more difficult passages should be interpreted. Some attempts have been ludicrous in the extreme. Yet none should lightly abandon the allegorical interpretation until they have read Hudson Taylor's *Union and Communion*, which illustrates the real spiritual riches that may be won in this way.[1]

There are many, however, who feel that this allegorical approach does not really do justice to the vividness and pure passion of the poem. So they prefer to think of it rather in terms of typology. In other words, it is a true love poem of people who really existed, but it describes a love which God was well pleased to take as a picture of His. Young, in his *Introduction to the Old Testament*, dismisses this view quite unreasonably out of hand. There is no parallel for allegory on such a scale in the Bible. In its relatively rare use, as in Ezekiel, we are left in no doubt of the fact that it is allegory.

In more modern times until recently the most popular interpretations have assumed that it is a drama. Some have seen two main characters in it, Solomon and the bride, others three, Solomon, the bride and the shepherd lover to whom she remains loyal in spite of all the allurements of the royal harem. Though both these interpretations can be spiritually most satisfying, it has been impossible to prove that ancient Israel knew such dramas. The same criticism applies with even more force to the 'liberal' suggestion that it is derived from pagan cult dramas.

Most moderns see in it a series of marriage poems. In other words, in this view they are not the expression of romantic love, but the rejoicing of a husband and wife in the joy and the

[1] Published by the Overseas Missionary Fellowship.

love God has given them. If we are tempted to find the language over frank, that is due to the corruption of our age. Provided we are prepared to use them typologically as well, this seems to be the most satisfactory approach. The Bible has something to say to all states and aspects of human life. So here we have its praise of true, pure married love, but we must not forget that it draws its power and meaning from a deeper and purer love, which it foreshadows.

RUTH

We know neither by whom this little book was written nor for what purpose. A comment like that in 4: 7 shows that it cannot have reached its present form for some considerable time after the events described. The allegorizer and dealer in types find much in it to exercise their ingenuity on, but I cannot help feeling that they are wasting their time. The beauty of the story is sufficient justification for its presence in Scripture, and the loyal love which breathes through it in all its parts can be used as an analogy of loyal love everywhere, whether it is God's or man's.

It had its special place in the Hebrew Bible, because it stood at all times as a guarantee of the right of the Gentile proselyte to find his place within in the people of God. For us too it should speak of the lack of rules and regulations that should exist for one who has come 'to take refuge under the wings of the God of Israel'.

LAMENTATIONS

Tisha b'Ab, the black fast – the Day of Atonement is the white fast – commemorates the destruction of both first and second Temple. The choice of Lamentations for reading in the service is too obvious to call for further mention or justification.

The book consists of five dirges or lamentations written in the years immediately following the destruction of Jerusalem and its temple by Nebuchadnezzar. There is no compelling reason for attributing them all to the same author. The only one we can possibly attribute to Jeremiah is the third, and even here the assumption is hazardous. The heading in our standard translations is based on the Septuagint and Talmudic tradition, but not on the Hebrew, which gives no indication of authorship.

The chief arguments against authorship by Jeremiah are the sense of shock and hopelessness which we can hardly attribute to the prophet, for from the first he had known what was coming. The most striking feature of the book is that the first four poems show an alphabetic acrostic, while the fifth has twenty–two verses, the number of letters in the Hebrew alphabet. The purpose was probably to keep the writer's overflowing grief and anguish within bounds, while containing the suggestion that here we have the whole of human grief portrayed from A to Z.

Though the author or authors were clearly familiar with Jeremiah and his teaching, they had the same experience as the disciples in the New Testament after the crucifixion of Christ. In the shock of loss they forgot the promise of restoration. God was well pleased to recognize that men can be overwhelmed by grief even while they continue to trust in Him, and so He permitted the expression of that grief to find its place in Scripture.

Those of us who have never had to pass through such an experience may readily claim that we should rejoice in the Lord at all times. We suggest that the joy of the Lord is our strength and that it is always available to us. The facts of human experience show, however, that the clouds of grief may settle down on even the choicest of the saints, making the Lord seem very far off and laming all Christian endeavour. It is then that Lamentations comes into its own. It does not clear the clouds, but it does assure the mourner that God understands and accepts his grief.

ESTHER

This is superficially the most contentious book in the Old Testament. It is not surprising that it is not mentioned in the New, and it is very doubtful whether the feast of Purim is either. There are grounds for thinking that the Qumran sectarians did not accept it; at least no fragment of the book has been found in the Dead Sea caves. This may, however, be due to pure accident.

Martin Luther, when speaking about 2 Maccabees, said, 'I am so hostile to this book and to Esther that I could wish that they did not exist at all, for they Judaize too greatly and have much pagan impropriety.' He has been echoed by many since then. Attention is drawn to the fact that the name of God is not mentioned in the book, though 'from another place' (4: 14) is undoubtedly an oblique reference to Him. There is a mention of fasting but not of prayer (4: 16). Mordecai was an assimilationist with a pagan name, as is also Esther's. He was quite willing that his niece should live in a pagan harem, and when it came to the moment of crisis, he was quite content that she should risk her life. The vengeance of the Jews (9: 1–15) has repeatedly and rightly proved a stumbling block to thoughtful Christians though it has been exaggerated.

In the Bible we frequently find reports of what happened without any comment on the rightness or wrongness of what is recorded. Esther is an outstanding example of this. Neither praise nor blame is given to any of the characters. What we are expected to learn is that God maintains His covenant loyalty to His people, even when their representatives happen to be at their most unattractive. He acts in grace, not according to man's worthiness. Indeed there is not even a suggestion that Mordecai's rudeness to Haman by which he put his own life and the existence of his people in jeopardy had any worthy or spiritual motive.

We sometimes meet the argument that the series of dramatic coincidences by which the tables are turned are a sign that the story cannot be true. Truth is often stranger than fiction, and the series of what we call coincidences was intended to show that God was acting without any conscious help from men.

So Esther too plays its part in the totality of God's revelation. It brings us the assurance of the certainty of the promise, 'On this rock I will build My church, and the powers of death shall not prevail against it.' We all too often wash out the history of the mediaeval church, as though it represented a period of pure apostasy. Again and again, however, we can see the power of God operative in it just as surely as it was in the time of Mordecai.

ELEVEN

Look to the Future

THE LAST THREE BOOK5 AMONG THE WRITINGS, AND SO IN THE Hebrew Bible, are Daniel, Ezra-Nehemiah and Chronicles, the last two becoming four in the Septuagint tradition, followed by the English translations. The force of Luke 11: 49–51 (Matt. 23: 34, 35) would seem to be our 'from Genesis to Revelation', for Abel is the first of the martyrs and Zechariah the last of them mentioned by name in the Hebrew canon (2 Chron. 24: 20, 21). So the present order was well established by the time of our Lord.

DANIEL

When the Septuagint placed Daniel among the prophetic books, it was only following that carnal logic that influenced its arrangement of the Old Testament books throughout. There is in fact no real evidence for the often made statement that also in Hebrew Daniel once stood in the prophetic canon. Equally too the explanations for its present place, adduced by both liberals and conservatives, normally carry little conviction.

Matt. 24: 15, to say nothing of the repeated use of the book in Revelation, is sufficient evidence of its prophetic nature, even if the prophetic title is not given in it to Daniel himself. But what sort of prophecy is it? Three times over (8: 26; 12: 4; 12: 9) it is made clear that the visions had not been given to Daniel for his contemporaries. Other prophets had spoken to the men of their own time, and their words had been preserved under the guidance of the Holy Spirit for posterity; Daniel had been given his visions not for his contemporaries, but for generations yet to come. This is one of the many indications that the Inter-Testamental period was not one of revelation but of waiting for the fulfilment of the revelation already given. From the history of the text it appears as though it may not have been a very widely-known book until the first of the crises it envisaged, viz. the persecution by Antiochus Epiphanes, was at hand.

The tension between predestination and free will is not one created merely by the New Testament or Christian theologians. Repeatedly in the prophets we find the apparent contradiction between the call to human response and the certain working out of God's foreknowledge and choice. But in them we always have the feeling that the prophet's appeal is a real one; the possibility of acceptance or rejection is always there (cf. Jer. 18; 5–11). When we come to Daniel – and the same is true of Revelation – to all intents and purposes there is no appeal to those who hear. Man has refused his chance, and God is working out His will and purposes inexorably.

From time to time in the past Israel or the Church entered on a period when it seemed as though the proclamation of God's will was purposeless and that the wicked were having their own way. It may well be that we are entering on such a time today. It is for times like these that the apocalyptic books were given. They serve less to reveal God's will and character and far more to encourage the hard-pressed believer to stand fast.

This is made particularly clear by the narrative chapters in Daniel. They are not recorded to glorify Daniel and his friends, but to show that there is no possible situation where God cannot protect His own, if such is His purpose (Dan. 3: 16–18). It is only as we are fully convinced of God's all-sovereign power around us that we can profitably look at the future. The great weakness of most expositions of Daniel and Revelation in modern times has been that the expositor has all too often dissociated himself from that which he has affirmed must come to pass. Either he has moved the fulfilment out of his own lifetime, or he has affirmed that the Church cannot conceivably experience the horrors foretold.

How little Daniel's visions were given to enable the saints to foresee what would come on future generations is illustrated most strikingly by the prophecy of the Seventy

Weeks (9: 24–27). There is no evidence that any pious Jew in the first century B.C. or A.D. deduced from it that the advent of the Messiah was nigh at hand. This was hidden even from the men of Qumran, who seem to have made a special study of Daniel. They did recognize that they were in 'the last times', but their understanding was based on 'the signs of the times' and not on this prophecy. Still more remarkable is that the prophecy of the Seventy Weeks is not mentioned in the New Testament. One might have expected that it would have featured most prominently in the apostolic preaching to the Jews, but we look for it in vain. It is more important to know that the future is securely in the hands of God and that so are His children also than we should be able to foresee each step in the working out of His plans before it is taken.[1]

THE CHRONICLER

It is today virtually universally recognized that 1 and 2 Chronicles, Ezra and Nehemiah 7: 73–12: 30 were written by the same man – the remainder of Nehemiah is taken directly from his diary or memoirs. The writer may well have been Ezra, but since this is not provable, the custom has grown up of calling him the Chronicler. Since 2 Chron. 36: 22, 23 are identical with Ezra 1: 1–3a, it is also generally assumed that Ezra–Nehemiah were once part of Chronicles, the more so as 2 Chron. 36: 23 really ends in the middle of sentence.

If that is so, the only reasonable explanation why Ezra-Nehemiah stands before Chronicles in Hebrew would seem to be that the rabbis saw the importance of the former before they appreciated the spiritual purpose and value of the latter.

The Former Prophets from Joshua to Kings had sought to show how history was a revelation of God. The purpose of the Chronicler was very different. Writing probably about 400 B.C. or a little later he wanted to encourage the Jews in their despondency. They had indeed returned in part from the Babylonian exile and had been able to rebuild the Temple in Jerusalem, but every vestige of political freedom remained

---

[1] Those who are readiest to accept this prophecy as genuine prediction all too often fail to realize that two quite contrasting expositions are possible.

denied to them, and there was no sign of the re-establishment of the Davidic monarchy. The Chronicler saw clearly that in the history of Israel two things were inextricably intertwined, the Davidic dynasty and the Temple – not the Tabernacle! So he wrote a history of both, so that men might recognize that if the Temple had been restored, then a restoration of the monarchy might be confidently expected. What he did not realize was that the lack of a king really showed that the Temple was no more than a shell without glory, waiting for the coming king to give it a new meaning.

The writer has not hesitated to reproduce his many sources in his own words, so creating a style that can easily be recognized by those that can read Hebrew. But when he uses material from Samuel and Kings, he normally quotes verbally accurately, thereby showing that he recognized these books as Scripture and implying that his own work should be interpreted in their light.

There have always been two elements in the Church. There are those who look for the Holy Spirit's guidance from day to day. They are always willing to abandon the old and traditional and try something new. Indeed, the very fact that something is traditional is often for them a challenge to reject it. Then there are those who rejoice in the old and traditional and who do not see why it should be abandoned.

These two attitudes are, of course, extremes, and most believers find themselves somewhere in between. For all that, when it comes to a decision, most will find themselves in one party or the other. For both the work of the Chronicler has a valuable message, for he holds the balances fairly between them. He makes no secret of the fact that monarchy and Temple were innovations. The failure of Saul, the first king, is clearly hinted at by the mention of his death (1 Chron. 10). Equally God's rebuke through Nathan of the whole Temple concept is recorded (1 Chron. 17: 4–6). Yet, by giving not merely the genealogies of Israel, but also of mankind, he anchors the new developments firmly in the history of the past. Whether or not God would have used king and temple had Israel been completely loyal to Him, we are not told, and it is immaterial, but having instituted them, He proceeded to use them. They became His will, and none had the right to alter them until God Himself should change or abolish.

On the other hand the power of the Spirit and man's simple

trust are repeatedly stressed. It is not the fact that he is the Lord's anointed that makes the king a blessing and a Saviour, but that he seeks the will of God and does it. We see priests and Levites as spiritual leaders and saviours, but that is when the Spirit of God comes upon them. So far is the Chronicler from being a friend of the ritualist, that the prophet plays a far larger part in his history of Judah than he does in the parallel narrative in Kings.

So the Old Testament closes, not with Malachi, as is so often suggested, but with the story of a people rebellious yet mercifully moulded by the grace of God through the institutions He had appointed. We see the bitter fruit of sin in exile, but we are also allowed to see the first light of a new dawn. Day had not yet come for the king of kings had not yet appeared, but the Temple stood as a token of God's grace and loyalty to His promises.

Since Cyrus had done the work which God had foretold of him, then assuredly the Servant of the Lord would come in due course to perfect God's work in Zion.

A comparison of Ezra 2: 1–70 with Neh. 7: 6–73, which should be identical, will show many interesting divergencies both in the spelling of the names and in the numbers. The main differences are indicated in the RV mg. of Ezra 2. This ought to be sufficient to indicate that those who copied the work of the Chronicler did not always show the same care as was exercised with the older books. Hence the reader should not create too many difficulties for himself by trying to reconcile the spelling of names and the size of numbers where they disagree with those in Samuel and Kings. Though he is not likely to want to pursue the subject, the differences should also make him realize that Hebrew script was in some particulars open to misreading, and this to some extent explains the textual alterations in RSV and NEB.

APPENDIX 1

Allegory, Typology and Analogy

WHEN THE STATEMENTS IN CH. 3 ON ALLEGORY WERE FIRST published, they produced considerable opposition and a correspondence which showed in some cases a slipshod use of technical terms, sometimes an unthinking acceptance of traditional exegesis from the narrow circles in which the writers moved.

Allegory is far older than Christianity. It was known and practised by the Palestinian rabbis and reached its height among the Jews of Alexandria, but before them had been used by the Greeks, especially in their treatment of Homer. Through the church in Alexandria allegory became firmly rooted in Christendom.

Origen (A.D. 182–251) affirmed that Scripture had three levels of truth (often a fourth was added): (a) The literal, or fleshly sense; (b) The moral sense; (c) The pneumatic or spiritual sense. Of these only the last was of any real value to the spiritual man. While he did not deny the truth of the first two, he emptied them of true value.

The evil of allegory lies in its turning its back on the Biblical story or teaching and refusing to allow them to speak directly to us. Instead it reads into them the allegorist's own thoughts, which, however high and noble, are not God's. One example must suffice. In Lk. 10: 30–37 we have a story, real or imaginary, which clearly teaches us our duty to our fellow-men. In the hands of St. Augustine we see Adam leaving the heavenly city for mortality. The devils and his angels stripped him of his immortality, persuaded him to sin and brought him to the verge of death. The priesthood and the ministry of the Old Testament could not help him, but the Samaritan (meaning Guardian, and hence our Lord) restrained his sin, giving him comfort and exhortation to work (oil and wine). The donkey was His human flesh, and being set on it meant believing in the incarnation. The inn is the Church, the innkeeper is the Apostle Paul, and the two pence are the promise of this life and the next. All this may be theologically true, but it has nothing to do with our Lord's teaching.

The nearest approach to the allegorical use of the Old Testament in the New is Gal. 4: 22–26. But it should be noted that it derives its force from the truth of the Genesis story. Paul is claiming to draw out the spiritual principle underlying what really happened. We are really dealing with an extreme case of analogy.

Typology is based on the New Testament conviction that certain ceremonies and historical happenings in the Old were ordained or so overruled by God that they might point to a greater reality to come. The treatment of the Tabernacle, its sacrifices and priesthood by Hebrews is an example of the first. Jonah (Matt. 12: 39, 40), the Israelites in the wilderness (1 Cor. 10: 1–11), the crossing of the Red Sea (1 Cor. 10: 1, 2) or Noah's flood (1 Pet. 3: 20, 21) are examples of the second. The use of Melchizedek in Heb. 7: 1–3 is based on the manner in which the Holy Spirit caused the Genesis story to be written.

Since typology, in contrast to allegory, stresses the reality of the happenings it deals with, it is to be commended, if it is used with restraint. We must, however, beware of finding types where they do not exist; it may be well to confine ourselves to those sections which the New Testament claims may be used as types, else there is the very real danger that the literal meaning is ignored.

The commonest use of Old Testament stories both in the New Testament and in sound Christian exegesis would seem to be not typology but analogy. The basic idea behind analogy is that since all has been created by God there will be similarities in creation on all its levels. Equally, evil will show itself in essentially similar ways on whatever level it appears. This is the justification for Christ's parables based on nature or on normal human behaviour, and for using life under the Old Covenant as illustrations of the higher levels of the New. So the good man under the Old will in measure foreshadow the perfect man of the New, and He in turn will be mirrored in the justified community of the Church. It is in this sense that we may so often use stories of the Patriarchs.

There is one peril in a careless use of analogy. While God's creation mirrors its Creator, He is infinitely high above it. That is why no Bible character is a type of God the Father, and why we must show great reserve in finding types of the Son. Analogies, unless we are very careful, will equally tend to give us false concepts of God, and it is in this way that some of the worst sins of the Church have been falsely justified.

The Order of the Old Testament Books in Hebrew

1. The Torah: The Five Books of Moses
2. The Nebi'im (Prophets):

The Former
{
Joshua
Judges
Samuel
Kings
}

The Latter
{
Isaiah
Jeremiah
Ezekiel
The Twelve
}

3. The Ketubim (Writings):
Psalms
Proverbs
Job

Megillot
{
Song of Songs
Ruth
Echah (Lamentations)
Qohelet (Ecclesiastes)
Esther
}

Daniel
Ezra-Nehemiah
Chronicles

Index